L.O.V.E.

Ladies
Operating
Very
Effectively

Finding the Power to Change Your World

DIANNE SHORTÉ

THREE BLACK DIAMONDS PRESS

L.O.V.E., Ladies Operating Very Effectively
©2016 Dianne Shorté

First Edition
Cover Design and Layout by: Richard R. Hefner
Edited by: Robin Quinn

All rights are reserved. No part of this book may be used or reproduced by any means—graphic, electronic or mechanical, including any photocopying, recording, taping or by any information storage retrieval system, without the written permission of the author except in the case of brief quotations under the "Fair Use Doctrine."

All quotations are respectfully included within the spirit of the Fair Use Doctrine, acknowledging the original source or author where known. As such, the author of this nonfiction work has used excerpts for purposes of illustrating or furthering the general theme of a chapter and/or the book.

Printed in the United States of America

ISBN: 978-0-9969913-0-8

Three Black Diamonds Press
369 S. Doheny Dr., Suite 1400
Beverly Hills, CA 90211
threeblackdiamondspress.com
info@threeblackdiamondspress.com

This book is dedicated to every young girl or woman
who ever asked the questions,
"Who am I?" and
"What is my purpose?"

Contents

Foreword v
Introduction vi
Characteristics of a Lady Operating Very Effectively (L.O.V.E.) xi
Chapter 1   You Can Do More Than You Think You Can 1
Chapter 2   Move Beyond Your Past 10
Chapter 3   Be Understanding 15
Chapter 4   Authenticity 21
Chapter 5   At Your Service 28
Chapter 6   The Power in a Woman 34
Chapter 7   L.O.V.E. and Happiness 39
Chapter 8   If The Gift Fits, Wear It 43
Chapter 9   Money Matters 48
Chapter 10   L.O.V.E. and Fear are Enemies 53
Chapter 11   Wisdom Is A Gift 58
Chapter 12   Getting Comfortable With Confrontation 63
Chapter 13   Your Vision Leads To Your Destiny 68
Chapter 14   Watch Your Mindset 73
Chapter 15   What's Holding You Back? 78
Chapter 16   Discover Your Strengths 85
Chapter 17   L.O.V.E. and Marriage 88
Chapter 18   Your Joy is in Your Journey 94
Chapter 19   Now It's Your Turn 101
Bibliography 103
Recommended Reading 105
Acknowledgments 106
About The Author 108

Foreword

Women all over the world serve as the life breath of their families, churches, jobs, and communities. Unfortunately, because of the multiple roles women play, many may suffer from poor mental, physical, social, and spiritual health. In L.O.V.E., Ladies Operating Very Effectively, the author Dianne Shorté, gives nuggets of wisdom that are proven to help them operate more effectively in every area of their lives. When we operate more effectively, we enjoy better health and overall well-being. Ms. Shorté's approach is simple, yet powerful as she gently guides you through the valley of health and wholeness. In *L.O.V.E., Ladies Operating Very Effectively,* Ms. Shorté shares her own stories and life lessons that helped her to become equipped to write this important book. She also highlights the strength of other women who have successfully overcome tragedy, trauma, and trouble in their lives, and are now operating effectively. L.O.V.E. Ladies Operating Very Effectively is a must read for women and the men who love them. In essence, Ms. Shorté has provided the necessary tools for women to live their best lives. When women are healthy they will raise up a nation of healthy women and girls. Thank you Dianne Shorté for teaching us all how to operate more effectively.

Gloria Morrow, Ph.D.
Licensed Clinical Psychologist
GM Psychological Services, Inc.

Introduction

Throughout the life of a woman, she will struggle to understand love, to find love, and to keep love. This book will not only help you reach each of these admirable goals, but it will also help you become L.O.V.E. "What is "L. O. V. E?" My definition for L.O.V.E. is simply "Ladies Operating Very Effectively." My dream is that this book becomes a blessing to everyone who reads it, and that it will inspire every woman to operate very effectively in every area of her life.

I'd like to provide a little background on how I arrived at the title and my company. It began with one of the most recognized words in the English language, "LOVE." Love is one of my favorite words, and I've always been enamored with the idea of love and the passion that the word love evokes. So it's no coincidence that "L.O.V.E." would become the title of my first book.

I have devoted my life to studying how women can discover their passions and live their dreams—how to inspire them to use their power to create the life that they have always wanted. My organization is specifically dedicated to help all women create a life that is purposeful, productive and powerful, always moving forward with authenticity, understanding, optimism, spirituality, health and living forgiveness. A life that is…L.O.V.E. This book was written to motivate and inspire you to change unproductive patterns of behavior, to develop effective habits, and to live your authentic life.

An Early Interest

My passion for women's issues began when I was young. Growing up in a single-parent household in a neighborhood in

East Palo Alto, California, I saw my mother and other women struggle to find a balance between self, family and their own desires. My mother was a classy, but troubled woman with an eighth-grade education who worked three jobs to provide a home for her three children. Like many women, my mother's real issues surfaced during her relationships and in child-rearing. I saw many women struggle to find a balance between home, work, creativity and family. It was during this time that I began to think about the qualities and attributes that would allow a woman to live a life that is meaningful, satisfying and honorable; one that would allow her to be content with her personal life even though her circumstances were difficult—a life that honored who she was created to be and what she was born to do. I was determined to become a successful woman and live my dreams by any positive means necessary. I was resolute about being a woman who takes care of her health, achieves her life goals, helps her community, raises well-adjusted and healthy children, and enjoys time with her friends and special man. I also wanted to inspire and motivate other women to do the same.

You'll Be Meeting Extraordinary Women

The extraordinary women featured in this book have been selected because they exemplify the qualities characterized in the acronym L.O.V.E. Some of them are single and devoted to their careers, and some are married and are very capable of balancing home and family, while still making time to be creative and give back to their communities. A few are celebrities who have masterfully melded their career and home life. These women are not perfect, but they share the ability to sacrifice for others, be transparent, self-correct, and make strategic changes as needed to achieve a well-rounded balance between self, family and community.

These women are powerful! Yet the impact they are making on their families, society and the world is often ignored and underestimated. The media recognizes community leaders and celebrities for their contributions, and while their reach may be newsworthy, broad and effective, it can sometimes lack the rich intimacy that the efforts of local women of power can provide. It's easier to help when you're a celebrity and have access to financial resources, and it's more challenging when you lack money and media contacts. These local women, like soldiers fighting a war they did not create, are in the trenches, teaching, serving and caring for the lives and struggles of women and children in their communities.

At the same time, there are some celebrity women at the ground level leading the way as L.O.V.E. Examples of such women include:

- **Michelle Obama**, leading the cause for wives of servicemen and getting children active and fit through her "Let's Move" campaign

- **Angelina Jolie**'s humanitarian causes and her proactive approach to health and wellness

- **Oprah Winfrey** through her Leadership Academy for Girls in South Africa

Though I have included these exceptional celebrities in the book, one of my main goals is to celebrate and make celebrities of the extraordinary "ordinary" women who are doing amazing work in their community and in the world—women who should be recognized nationally and internationally. These women should inspire you to dream BIG and reach deep to utilize your full potential.

Get Ready to Walk in Your Power!

Together we are going to do the work required for you to live the life that you were created to live—the life that you really want! Your dreams matter and they are important. There is NOTHING that can get in your way but you! I am a living testimony that there is Power in a Woman...the Power to overcome any circumstance and make it work for you and others...the Power to change your environment and the world. Let's get busy so you can become L.O.V.E., one of the Ladies Operating Very Effectively!

Characteristics of a Lady Operating Very Effectively (L.O.V.E.)

She **Is** Proactive.
She **Is** Courageous.
She **Is** Optimistic.
She **Is** Balanced.
She **Is** Spiritual.
She **Is** Respected.
She **Is** Loving.
She **Is** Forgiving.
She **Is** Purposeful.
She **Is** Secure.
She **Is** Healthy.
She **Is** Beautiful.
She **Is** Understanding.
She **Is** a Mentor.

She **Has** a Sense of Freedom.
She **Has** Perspective.
She **Has** a Passion to Affect the Lives of Others.
She **Has** Focus.
She **Has** Strength.
She **Has** Faith.
She **Has** Peace.
She **Has** Patience.
She **Has** Self-Control.

She **Can** Communicate Effectively.
She **Can** Inspire and Motivate Others.
She **Can** Achieve Her Life Goals.

She **Will** Impact the World!

Chapter 1
You Can Do More Than You Think You Can

Your capability to "do more" is dependent on your ability to recognize your gifts, strengths and to make strategic connections to further your dreams. It also depends on your trust and belief in yourself. Some of you have relegated your lives to mundane existences. There is nothing wrong with this type of living unless you have a burning desire that there be a greater purpose for your life.

The idea of doing more is not about spending more time on menial tasks such as posting selfies on Facebook, checking for likes; cleaning the house, washing the laundry, or organizing the shoes in your closet. It is about knowing yourself and determining what you're born to do, what you want most in life, and what you are willing to do to obtain it. You may actually have to let the dishes pile up or go on a social media diet and learn to be still. I constantly struggle in this area. I will clean the house, wash and fold the laundry, make the bed and then sit down to do "something important." Next thing you know, I've run out of steam. The point is that we should focus on the priorities because we will always have time for the little things.

Michelle Obama is a perfect example of a woman who has used her influence to do more. Rather than sit idly on a throne as the First Lady of the United States, she has used her status to impact the lives of millions. Michelle has championed the cause for wives and families of those who serve in the armed forces, and she started Let's Move, a national campaign to encourage parents, school districts and communities to provide children with healthy food and to eradicate childhood obesity. This is what it means to do more. She is not required to do anything but support her husband and raise her own family. It is her soul and spirit that recognizes we all need help and those in a position to help should answer the call.

We have all heard stories about women who have performed miraculous feats. There's the mother who lifted a car to rescue her child who was pinned underneath it, the woman who single-handedly raised five children, with all of them graduating from college, and the woman who survived a deadly stabbing and forgave her attacker. These women operate from a place of strength, grit and the belief that you must do what needs to be done.

Questioning Our Abilities

I would bet that at some point in their lives each of the women I've mentioned so far questioned her ability to do what she was later able to accomplish. As women, we tend to be insecure about our true abilities. In the book, *The Confidence Code*, authors Katty Kay and Claire Shipman state:

> *...what we need to do is start acting and risking and failing, and stop mumbling and apologizing and prevaricating. It isn't that women don't have the ability to succeed, and that stops us from even trying. Women are so keen to get everything just right that we are terrified of getting something wrong. But if we don't take risks, we'll never reach the next level.*

Their studies and research are very comprehensive and some of it was surprising, but understandable. I identify with what Katty and Claire say about our aversion to taking risks. There are many things that I would have attempted when I was younger if I had allowed myself to possibly fail. I would have studied to be a medical doctor, a teacher, a sports psychologist, a professional singer, a dancer on Broadway or a television announcer. Although my career choice to be a legal secretary was the fulfillment of a dream—it was the safe option. It didn't require me to train or study for years, nor did it create the flutter of fear that wells up inside of you when you reach past your comfort zone.

To pursue the risky dreams would have been to go against everything my mother wanted for my life. My mother, despite having only an eighth grade education, was able to get steady work. Mom was consistently employed as a waitress at a prestigious hotel, and she drove school buses for several school districts. She believed that if you got a job you would be secure. She was correct, to a degree.

Following the advice of my mother, I got a job in the ninth grade, and I have had a job ever since. It wasn't until I was much older that I began to take risks, to do those things that were close to my heart and to go after the "scary dreams." I'm not talking about those bad nighttime dreams that leave you afraid after watching a movie thriller, but the dreams that seem so lofty you think you might die trying to achieve them. The thought of these goals can evoke intense emotion when you think of others who are living your goal/dream, and you experience a tinge of envy or jealousy. These feelings are actually your call to action. Start now; don't wait too long to begin. No matter what anyone tells you, there is a window of opportunity that will close if you wait too long.

Surprised by Our Success

I've heard many successful women say that they're surprised by their own success. They start with a desire, which leads them to make certain choices, and in time, success is both their result and their reward. Of course, the actual route to their success was not as simple, and it evolved in a much more complex way. An actress may endure an enormous amount of rejection before she succeeds, a doctor suffers through eight years plus of training, and a pilot spends thousands of hours in study and flight to soar through the sky. As you probably have discovered, getting from where you are to where you want to be is like traveling on a two-lane road through mountainous terrain. The road twists and turns, ascends and descends, and at some point you wonder if you'll ever arrive at your destination.

As a dancer, I can totally relate. Dancers spend years and years studying and training their bodies to achieve a measure of expertise. At each point, you are challenged to go beyond your previous level. When a dancer perseveres through pain, uncertainty and insecurity, she arrives at her desired goal. However, the irony of physical activity is that every day is different. One day you may be able to hit the perfect pirouette, but three days later you can't seem to get the perfect alignment. You tell yourself to pull up, press down, engage your core, keep your shoulders down, prepare to spot in the direction that you're turning, and don't forget to point your toes. Then off you go and halfway into the turn, you fall over.

Falling over as a dancer or hitting the wrong note as a singer is the beginning of achieving the perfect three-turn pirouette or reaching the highest note in your register. There is no success without struggle. Life has taught me that the work we put into learning a new task, achieving a goal, reaching a level of professional success, or perfecting an old talent is exactly what is needed to get in a position to be and to do more than we think we can.

Your ability to do more is created by a number of factors: desire and motivation, commitment and hard work, and patience. Ask yourself if the thing you want to accomplish is important enough that you will weather any storm to complete it. I was reluctant to title this chapter "You Can Do More Than You Think You Can" for fear that some of you might use it to run yourself into the ground by working too much, thinking too much, texting too much, Facebooking too much, helping others too much, or doing any number of things too much. We women tend to "do the most" *(slang for doing anything extreme)* and many times our efforts are directed in the wrong direction.

Women workaholics are good at justifying their overexertion but do so at the expense of their health, relationships, and even their sanity. We all know them. They are willing to sacrifice their children, friendships and marriages for a career. Chasing a dream of success at the expense of what matters most is neither smart nor wise. Hopefully, you're not one of these women. Workaholics spend long hours being busy, neglect their children and partners, but rationalize it by telling themselves that the family would go hungry if they didn't work three jobs. They don't have time to visit with relatives or friends and their excuse is that they have goals to achieve and responsibilities to take care of. Many of us have used the same excuse; I definitely have. But in defense of those of us who are more balanced, I must point out that our work life doesn't threaten the fabric of our relationships. My respect for Iyanla Vanzant grew immensely when she admitted on national television that as a parent she had been a good provider but a terrible mother. It takes a lot to speak the truth and doing so will empower you to be more than you think you can be.

Of course, you may be checking everything off your list

and doing a lot of things you are convinced are necessary and important. But as it has been said, "All movement is not progress." I want you to focus on the capacity that you have at a deeper level to do more than you believe you can do.

My Story

After my mother died when I was 20 years old, I struggled with how to take care of myself financially and continue my education. The Social Security payments were not enough to cover my living expenses, and I had not qualified for financial aid. I had the bright idea to apply for some form of aid from the welfare department to fill in the gap. This was incredibly uncomfortable for me because my mother had been a very proud woman, and she had worked three jobs so that she would not have to ask anyone for help. We were raised to be independent (which meant *don't ask anyone for anything*). It wasn't until years later that I learned about interdependence at a much deeper level. I will cover this in another chapter because it's very important to your success and your ability to succeed that you learn interdependence.

This encounter with the welfare department was one of those life-altering experiences, the type that gives you the opportunity to make a decision that truly changes your direction. You will make many of these decisions in your lifetime, and hopefully you will do so with conviction, courage and wisdom. You will have to trust yourself.

So what happened at the welfare office? Well, after I brought them every piece of paper they required—such as the phone bill, the electricity bill, my mother's death certificate, etc.—one day I returned with the final piece of paper, or so I thought. The woman behind the counter looked at me with disdain and told me (not asked me) to bring her one more document. I can't even remember what it was. What I do remember is that I felt mortified at how she was treating me, sad that I didn't have any parents, and was at the mercy of a system that was designed to assist people.

I went home and cried for hours. When I stopped crying, I made a decision that I would never ask anyone for help. I would take care of myself. Although I was frightened and unsure of what life would hold for me, I went into action. Motivated by embarrassment, pride and dignity, I walked into a law firm with a dream of a career in the legal field and applied for a job for which I had neither training nor experience. My decision set me on the path to a very fulfilling and lucrative career, which afforded me the resources to live out all of my dreams and goals.

Meet Corliss Bennett-McBride...

In high school, Corliss Bennett-McBride set her eyes on one of the most prestigious private colleges in the United States, the University of Southern California (USC). The process for completing college applications is hard work for everyone, and Corliss was only an average student. She did not have the high SAT scores necessary to get accepted to USC. Knowing this, she worked hard her senior year to raise her GPA to a higher number, and did get accepted. This was just the beginning. While attending USC, Corliss got a job there, working her way up. She became the Director for the Center for Black Cultural and Student Affairs, and continued her education. While working on her doctorate, she was diagnosed with cancer and was forced to take a leave of absence. In true Corliss fashion, she endured the grueling treatments, and is now cancer-free for seven years. She completed her doctorate.

A few years ago, I took my son to hear Corliss speak to a group of high school students and their parents. I was so enamored with her charisma, passion and energy that I went back to school.

Corliss is captivating, engaging and memorable as a motivational speaker. She exudes an air of competence, while being personable and willing to help others. In the true spirit of LO.V.E., Corliss continues to inspire, motivate and help students get into USC.

Audra Bryant—Moving Past the Pain

There are those times in life when your dreams get crushed, so what do you do? Audra Bryant, a beautiful and talented young girl, was engaged to be married to the person she believed to be the man of her dreams. Unfortunately, the engagement was called off and she began to nurse her pain. Audra experienced a brief period of depression until she was struck with the idea to write a play, which she had always dreamed of doing. Within a year of writing the play, she held auditions and cast the play, found a masterful director (my husband), and opened to a full house in a 99-seat theatre.

Audra is a talented singer and actress, and she has a bright future in front of her. She continues to realize that she is more than the other half to a marriage and that her value far exceeds the rejection of one man. If your relational situation is on a downturn, you should know that it is temporary, and also that there is so much more that life is expecting from you.

S-t-r-e-t-c-h-i-n-g Ourselves

In 2014, my company, L.O.V.E., participated in the Entertainment Industry Foundation's 2014 Revlon Run/Walk for Women. After the run, one of my team members came to me, exuberant that she had finally walked over 3.5 miles in one day with her bad knee. Normally she only allowed herself to walk one mile per day, and then she would have to ice the knee. After her Revlon walk, realizing that she had actually walked over five miles that day, my team member saw that she had much more in her than she had realized. Like Corliss and Audra, she is an example of what can be achieved when women move in the direction of their passions and desires.

Start now to build your strength for your dreams. Discipline yourself now to live your best life. Legendary Coach Bear Bryant said, "It's not the will to win that matters, but the will to prepare to win that counts."

How can you prepare to access your ability to be more and to do more? Both Corliss and Audra knew they had the talent and the desire to achieve their goals. What they found along the way was their motivation.

What is your motivation to discover all that you can be and do? Is it to leave a legacy for your family? Do you want to inspire other people by your life? Maybe you want to change the world. You can do it. Talk with someone you admire.

Any time that you honor your dreams, you confirm that you are more than you think you are, and you can be more than you are now. During her fight with cancer, Corliss knew that if she could make it through that battle, she could achieve anything. She never gave up on her goal to complete her doctorate. Audra poured herself into a cathartic piece of art and compelling story that not only helped her heal, but also was healing to her audiences.

To be more of who you are and do more than you think you can, prepare yourself to take some risks, to exercise your courage, and to move out of your comfort zone.

DON'T ALLOW LIMITED THINKING TO UNDERMINE YOUR UNLIMITED ABILITY.

Chapter 2

Move Beyond Your Past

It doesn't matter whether our past was good or bad - on some level, our past is comfortable. It belongs to us and we subconsciously honor it. The irony is that our past can be our best friend (if we learn from it and move on) or our worst enemy (if we don't). Many of us have lived so long in the past that we are emotionally stuck there. Everyone has a past, even an infant. A pregnant mother who uses drugs creates a horrible past for the infant, whereas the perfect pregnancy creates a different past for a child.

Ironically, whether our past was happy or sad, we must learn to let go of it to realize our best life, in the present. Holding on to the past can create a pattern of thinking and behavior that is out of touch with the person who you have become or who you want to be. We tend to glamorize the past, even though it could have been tumultuous and painful. We hold a "Good Ole Days" mentality about the way things used to be.

Actually, most of us are in the dark as to how to line up our feelings about the future and the past. There are the single women who want to be married and are unaware that they are looking for a replacement for the father who was perfect in every way. There are married women who are expecting their husband to run the household just like their father did and/or to be a better man than their absent father was. The problem is that neither of these types of women is aware of the fact that they are unconsciously setting themselves up for failure. What's happening is that they are subconsciously seeking comfort and safety in the familiarity of their pasts.

Taking a Deeper Look

In her book, *The Right Questions*, author Debbie Ford poses questions to help us make better choices to move from autopilot (an unconscious state of mind) to conscious thinking. One of those questions is: *"Will this choice propel me toward an inspiring future or will it keep me stuck in the past?"* Debbie says that we must become aware of the underlying commitments and conflicts that are fueling our behavior. These commitments and conflicts show up in our lives and create conflicting behaviors, which keep us from achieving our goals. They actually sabotage our plans.

For example, let's say you want to get married and have a happy marriage. The most important thing you need to do is to prepare yourself mentally and emotionally for living with another person every day—24/7. Living together will mean giving up your personal space, sharing your closet (this was a tough one for me), embracing new relatives, sharing your personal financial information with another person, and so forth and so on. Of course, not many of us prepare in this manner. We plan for the events, such as the wedding (party) and the honeymoon (vacation), rather than the experience of being married.

Let's go back to the concept of underlying commitments and conflicts. Assuming that the reason most women want to get married is to "live happily ever after until death do you part," you'd think that we ladies would contemplate the real issues surrounding being a wife—like core values, personality compatibility, and mutual goals and beliefs. Well, the culprit that undermines your decisions is found in your past, and it has followed you right to the church in the example of getting married. Our past is like a magnet consistently pulling us back to where we are comfortable, and where we have far less fear because we know what to expect.

Free to Love, Free to Live

How many of you have stayed in a situation you knew would not be good for you but it was familiar and you knew that you could endure it? Have you put matters that are not important in front of things that matter most? Let me be the first to answer in the affirmative to both questions. Yet how wonderful would our lives be if we could move beyond our pasts and forget about the pain, heartbreak, failures and disappointments that have made us feel timid and insecure about reaching our dreams and goals? The key to changing is realizing that we are called upon to live in the present, and to create from wherever we are.

Think about it. You could be free to love again, free to create the life that you really want—not the one that you find acceptable to present to the world right now. In the areas of love and accomplishments, the past creeps in to take away our most cherished dreams for our future.

There are many women who are in relationships that are unfulfilling, and there are a staggering number of women who work at jobs that are not what they want to do. Would you let go of your past if you had that option? Are you aware of how you are allowing the past to impact your present, which in turn is affecting your future? Do you want to move beyond your past?

Start *today*—do not procrastinate. We procrastinate, at some level thinking we are not capable of doing whatever we are putting off. We procrastinate, when we are insecure. We procrastinate, when something in our past has created a thought pattern that keeps us "stuck." We procrastinate, even when we are on the precipice of change. Don't be fooled into thinking that you have unlimited time. The past can keep you from moving forward in your life. Time will continue to move forward while you stand still.

Opening to a New Landscape

To move beyond your past, you must learn to recognize when you are rationalizing behavior that is obviously getting in the way of your success. Our minds are very adept at creating stories to justify our hidden fears. I know a woman who so skillfully rationalizes her ineffective behavior that everyone except her can see how her lifestyle has become the reason she cannot meet her goals. She does not listen to others and has dug her heels in so deep that she is spinning out of control.

Moving beyond the past takes clarity of purpose, a willingness to ask the right questions of yourself, and a look at your behavior so you can achieve your dreams. Remember this: What you do today will be the past by tomorrow, and what you do tomorrow will determine your future. So the most important time in your life is the present moment because it is creating both your past and your present.

Use your past failures as signposts directing you to the right choices. Continue to fail, but learn from each failure. As a matter of fact, you should welcome each failure as motivation to move past your fear of making mistakes. Failure is simply doing the same thing over and over again, which has not previously worked in the past. You'll eventually find yourself where you want to be if you're willing to take an honest look at your choices and your behavior and ask yourself some very pertinent questions. David Richo, author of *When the Past Is Present*, says, "All of our ways of seeing the world are screened and stunted by our past until the rare moment of opening happens. Then a new landscape opens and we find our place in it." In other words, when you operate from a conscious place, you can see everything clearly.

A woman should use her past as a tool for growth and healing, and share her experiences to give hope to others. Sharing our mistakes and lessons helps others to learn how to make better decisions.

It's important to keep the past in proper perspective. We cannot afford to live in the past when it interferes with our present. Instead, use it to craft your present, along with strategies to achieve an exceptionally satisfying and fulfilling future.

YOUR PAST SHOULD BE THE ROADMAP TO A BETTER LIFE, NOT THE STUMBLING BLOCK.

Chapter 3
Be Understanding

It takes an open mind and heart to be an understanding person. The ability to stand in someone else's shoes takes learning how to be considerate of the other party's perspective. To listen with empathy and to have the ability to recognize the different emotional thought processes of another person is a skill worth developing, especially if you desire to have better relationships, own your own company, and be a good parent. In other words, when you learn to put yourself in someone else's shoes, you can empathize with their feelings.

When you can show empathy, you are positioned to hear and fully experience somebody's pain, sorrow or joy. Stephen Covey, author of *The 7 Habits of Highly Effective People*, puts it this way: "Empathic (from empathy) listening gets inside another person's frame of reference. You look out through it, you see the world the way they see the world, you understand their paradigm, you understand how they feel."

The definition of "understand" is to recognize the character of a situation, to grasp the meaning of what is occurring, and to accept it for what it is.

One of the hallmarks of a "lady operating very effectively" is her ability to be empathic to someone else's situation, to the degree that she can understand what another person may be experiencing. The issues and challenges women face are basically the same. When we can understand each other's struggle, we can better help each other succeed.

Meet Efuru Flowers…

Very few women embody the qualities of understanding and compassion like Efuru, which is demonstrated in her 24-year marriage. Efuru began to exercise that understanding while in college, when her parents divorced, and it was refined in year ten of her own marriage. Every marriage or important relationship eventually hits the point where it must be redefined, refined and realigned to address the needs, wants and desires of all involved.

When her marriage hit that rough patch around year ten, it was Efuru's understanding nature that led her to work through the challenges with her husband. Her keen ability led her to look at their struggles and recognize the part she played. She also recognized that her children would suffer if her marriage ended.

Over the years, Efuru has impacted and influenced the lives of many women with her wisdom and gentle spirit. She has helped me to see my blind spots and has given me insight into my shortcomings or shortsightedness. Whenever I want to make an important or life-changing decision, I look to her to give me guidance. There have been times when I chose not to take her advice, and I could have saved myself from a painful and difficult situation. But, as she would say, "Everyone has to make her own choices. The life she leads has to be on her terms, and she must go through whatever is necessary for her growth."

Learning Compassion

Throughout my teens and early twenties, I was not an empathetic person. I believed that life was black or white, and gray was just a cop-out. Being self-motivated and highly competitive, I was a force to be reckoned with. I didn't believe in excuses, and

I felt that everything we experienced was under our own control. I mean *everything*. I felt that whatever problem someone faced should not be hard to fix and that it just required hard work and stick-to-it-ness.

While my philosophy with respect to achieving goals was a good one, my ability to "stand under" (walk in someone's pumps) was severely limited by my lack of wisdom and life experience. As fate would have it, as I experienced pain, suffering and joyful situations, I began to feel what it would feel like to be exposed to various life situations. Each experience gave me greater understanding of the impact that life can have on someone.

For instance, when I was a teenager, my mother often embarrassed me when I got in trouble by coming to the school and cursing out a teacher in front of anybody who was in earshot. This taught me to have compassion for children whose parents scream at them in the grocery store or spank them in public. It's amazing to me how many parents feel this is acceptable behavior. I can understand how defeated they feel when their children act up but I believe that every moment is a teaching-learning moment. In this instance, the child is the teacher; they are teaching the parent to be patient and how to behave well in public, instead of embarrassing the child.

Higher Levels of Understanding

There are levels of understanding that only are possible with maturity and an understanding of human nature and human psychology.

My husband and I attended a marriage preparation course at our church before we were married. One of the recommendations from the course was that as a married couple we should associate with other Godly married couples. The idea is be friends with couples who are experiencing the same things and who have the same teaching with respect to marriage. This was not because of their expertise, but because they could understand the challenges and issues that are integral parts of marriage.

We now know several couples that we call when we need to vent and there are couples that call us. Many times in life, you will be forced to seek out the wisdom of someone who has been walking in the shoes that you want to wear, and it is very smart to get information and to ask for help if you need it.

Understanding in Families

One area where we should seek understanding is in helping our children find their place in the world. Many of us transfer the dreams we once had onto our children. Fortunately, God created our children with their own dreams and gifts, and a parent's goal should be to recognize her child's own talents and to help nurture the necessary skills that will help him or her succeed.

When we are operating effectively, our problems and issues can help us understand each other's problems. It's my opinion that God intends for us to learn compassion by experiencing troubles in our own lives. The newly wedded woman who previously raised her children alone can or should understand when her new husband's ex-wife calls their home to speak with her children's father. The single mom should understand being disrespected by the current partner of her ex because she herself could have experienced the same situation.

This area of blended families presents very difficult issues to navigate in the lives of women today. For instance, look at the complications of the single mother who has to share custody with the father of her children who is now in another relationship. Or perhaps your parents are still friends with your ex-husband or there's an ex-wife who wants to remain friends with her ex-husband's children. Relationships that are created as branches from previous marital relationships, or long-term associations, struggle to stay together and many times they cannot be sustained without understanding.

A funny story in my own family is when my mother became friends with my brother's ex-wife's boyfriend (the tangled webs we weave). My oldest brother's first wife was a sweet and kind woman who gave birth to my mother's first grandchild. When my brother divorced his wife (Wife #1), my mother did not stop caring for her and they remained very close friends. My brother's ex-wife eventually found a nice guy and started a relationship. Yes, you guessed it; the new boyfriend became a part of our family.

My brother was livid. He could not understand how we could embrace another man being with his ex-wife. The only explanation that I can offer about the way our family operated was that we weren't married to his ex-wife and therefore we didn't divorce her. Looking back, I now understand how I am very much like my mother in this regard. I am amiable with my exes, their exes and the children of all the exes.

Taking in Another's Perspective

One of my "school-of-life books" (books that I have used to transform my mind and my life) is *The Value in the Valley* written by Iyanla Vanzant. In her words, there is a Valley of Understanding where "we are provided an opportunity to strengthen our vision of how we see ourselves and others." She says that understanding is about acceptance and not forcing a situation into the hole where we want it to fit.

In other words, understanding requires us to learn how to listen without using our own life to filter what we hear and being at peace with what is. This is a tremendous challenge because we experience everything through our own colored glasses, if we are not self-aware. For example, your best friend might be having a problem with her boyfriend which appears to mirror the same problems you had with your ex-boyfriend. Your tendency, if you're looking through your life lens, would be to give her the same advice and strategy that you used—perhaps breaking up, sending an ugly photo of him over Instagram, or dogging him on out on Facebook. Even though your situations are similar, the reasons for your problems could be starkly different and the solution to your friend's issues could be simple and fixable or too complex to warrant a response from you. When giving advice, we must use wisdom and have the ability to remove our own agenda and our desire for any particular result. This is very difficult to do; I'm still working on this myself. I am learning to take into consideration all of the issues surrounding someone's situation and determining the best advice at that moment.

When we choose to understand other people, we are saying that we will look at their situation from their perspective and we will agree to accept what is. Today we are in a much more challenging time and understanding is crucial. The world has changed and, along the way, some of us have not. But one thing is certain, we will all be forced to change if we are to live in a way that allows us to sustain healthy familial relationships.

Same-sex marriages and sex changes alter the dynamics of how we relate to someone we knew. We will have to help young children understand why their mother lives with a woman now and how and why their uncle is no longer a man. We will all become better people as we exercise our ability to accept each other. The Bible says, "As much as possible, live at peace with all people." Learn to understand each other and to do this you need to start first with understanding yourself—your motives, your actions, your thoughts and your prejudices.

THE WOMAN WHO LACKS UNDERSTANDING WILL LEARN IT WHEN SHE NEEDS TO RECEIVE IT.

Chapter 4
Authenticity

My mother was a strict disciplinarian. Though not a church-going woman, she took the Bible to heart in terms of "spare the rod and spoil the child." She did not spare her rod when disciplining us. My mother beat me for every infraction, whether missing school, bad grades, or sneaking out of the house. Most of my beatings came as a result of my fighting in school. It seemed that the more she beat me, the more I fought at school.

Fighter with a Good Heart

In the elementary grades and high school, I had a terrible attitude with a personality to match. I was a lazy student and my grades reflected it. If I had to, I would classify the person I was during this period as "evil." The characters in the movie Mean Girls were mild compared to my behavior as an angry teen, and I'm embarrassed to share some of the things that I did.

Most of my friends' parents did not like me and I couldn't understand why. I was honest to a fault, loyal, kind and I had a good heart. I really loved people. I can hear you thinking, "Evil and angry are not synonymous with a good heart and loving people." Yet in my heart and soul, I had glimpses of my true self.

Because of my anger towards my mother, I was lashing out at others. My response to being hurt and hit was to hurt and hit others. Every person responds to pain and punishment differently and, for me, they only pissed me off and made me angrier. Of course, I had to vent that anger somewhere, so off to school I went and my anger and bitterness came with me. In my heart, I always knew that something was not right with my behavior and how I treated others but I was young and confused. I felt one way on the inside, yet struggled to get my behavior to match my heart. As I grew and matured, it became apparent to me that I had to find a way to get my behavior to match my heart and soul.

My life changed the day I realized that my anger and evil behavior were directly related to how I was being treated at home (knowledge is power). No longer did I feel like a confused misfit; I was now empowered to choose how I wanted to behave, and to become who I wanted to be. Several things became apparent to me, one being that I was a strong-willed person who wanted respect. The fighting at school was to get the respect that I didn't receive at home.

I can vividly remember the day that I felt the change in my heart. (The attitude and behavior modification took much longer.) That day, I was in the tenth grade sitting in class intently listening to the teacher, which was not my usual behavior. I felt alive and hungry to learn. My brain was fully engaged, and I heard my authentic self say, "I love learning." From that day forward, I set out on a journey to explore, embrace and nurture my authentic self—whatever she looked like and wherever that would lead me. Through many years of reading, therapy and education, plus hours of talking with my girlfriends, I began to put it all together. Lesson learned: Every new situation and challenge will present you with an opportunity to hone and define your authenticity.

Being Willing to Question Your Life

Another test of my authenticity occurred in my early thirties. I worked with an attorney who was rude, arrogant, pompous and had zero interpersonal skills. He was the type of person who never said "good morning" or "good night." His way of asking for his work to be done was borderline abusive. This man looked through you when he spoke to you and never acknowledged your presence around his peers. Throughout my career in the legal field, most of the attorneys with whom I worked treated me as a colleague, not like a second-class citizen. I tried to handle him by using my natural desire to serve others, all to no avail. This relationship reminded me of the abuse that I had endured from my mother. Consequently, I learned that my authentic self does not and will not accept abuse in any form from anyone.

After a year of working with this attorney, I concluded that I had to move on. I had to leave a job that I had loved. So, with a heavy heart, I began interviewing for new jobs. What happened next was the universe's way of confirming that my authenticity and commitment to my true self would be rewarded. My firm announced that we were moving to a new location, and the attorney that I worked with would be moving to another group within the firm. I didn't have to leave the job I loved, and as of the publication of this book, after 19 years, I am still employed there. And guess what? This attorney left over five years ago.

The main point of this story is that you must be willing to question a relationship, a friendship or a job if it doesn't reflect the true image of the person you are or the person you want to become. Oprah Winfrey quit her job as a television reporter because she didn't feel that it was in line with who she was at her core. She hated delivering the news and trying to pretend that the tragedies didn't bother her.

As one of Oprah's biggest fans, I have always felt that Oprah tries to merge together her spiritual/religious self and uses television as her forum to impact the world. I can remember when she would not use the word "God" on *The Oprah Winfrey Show*.

I knew that she was raised in the church and that she was being used by God to help so many others find their way to God. For instance, she has impacted my own life as I've watched her grow and evolve. Her keen ability to question her life, her thoughts and her actions has inspired me to ask myself the same questions, and the result of doing this has indeed been life-changing.

Becoming Authentic Takes Courage

If you're reading this book, you probably have a desire to identify your power and be effective and authentic. Ask yourself, "Who is my authentic self?" If you can't answer this right now, it's okay. By the time you finish this book, I am hoping you will have more clarity about your authentic self and what you are here to do.

What I have learned is that my authentic self is bold, brave and powerful. At some level, I have always known this. The angry young girl who spoke up for herself and fought for her identity as a teenager (albeit negatively) is the same woman who graduated from college with honors while raising two sons as a single parent and working a full-time job as a legal secretary. That same angry young girl started an entertainment business, Simply Samba Entertainment, which resulted in work with such clients as Ronald and Nancy Reagan, Will Smith, Nicollette Sheridan, Maurice Marciano, Merv Griffin, Debbie Allen, the Los Angeles Philharmonic and others.

Getting to authenticity takes courage and that courage is usually needed right smack in the middle of a challenge. The challenge is just the test for you to practice being authentic amidst the storm. As Brene Brown, author of *I Thought It Was Just Me (but it isn't)*, says, "Every minute is an opportunity to practice authenticity." What she proposes is that every person chooses to be authentic or not. When making the choice to honor your true feelings rather than avoiding the discomfort of not meeting other people's expectations, you are embracing the right choice and your authentic self.

Ways to Explore Your Authenticity

It's not easy to look honestly at your life and see your shortcomings. However, you must do the work to become authentically you. Why? Because your life depends on it. How do you become your authentic self? Start by answering the following questions:

- What do you know and feel in your heart and soul about yourself?
- Do you see a pattern of inconsistent behaviors?
- Are you happy with the person that you present to the world?
- Are your relationships genuine?
- Are you a people-pleaser?

Ultimately, the key to tapping into your authentic self is to recognize what makes you feel complete, peaceful and honest. For me, I have always felt very content and at peace when I am talking with people, counseling a friend about a relationship, or listening to someone share their pain.

You can get a glimpse into your authentic self by thinking about the people you respect and admire and by talking with your friends. Your close friends oftentimes, not always, know more about you than you recognize about yourself.

One of my clients, a 44-year-old, single, beautiful lady is a perfect example of a woman who struggled with authenticity. She didn't know what she wanted to do with her life and ended up wandering through her twenties and thirties taking menial jobs, staying in relationships that were not what she wanted, and failing to follow her passion or chase her dreams. Why? Because she didn't realize her talents and gifts could become her career.

One of the most difficult life challenges is to know yourself at your core. What do you need to be happy? What turns you on? Where do you draw the line with relationships? Her familial issues caused this woman to struggle with owning and accepting herself, and her true desires—which involved knowing what she felt and what she wanted at any given time. She also had a major flaw that paralyzes many women from growing into their best selves; that flaw is the failure to listen to wise counsel. A friend of mine used to say that if three people who don't know each other, but all know you, say the same thing about you than you can believe it to be true. Being honest with yourself about yourself is not possible without feedback from others.

It's also important to be mindful of your life and to evaluate yourself based on your relationships, what you do, and how you act. It is definitely a challenge to address your blind spots or inner demons, but in doing so you can release a powerful energy that can propel you toward the goals that are truly your life direction. We believe that others cannot see the truth of what is really going on with us. Yet our choices and actions telegraph to others what is really going on inside. The key to your truth will be found as you continue to look deeper within yourself and make daily choices that support your authentic self. Ask people who are close to you to help you see the blind spots in your personality. It's amazing what others know about you that you cannot see.

I recommended that my client begin her journey to authenticity by only pursuing those things that make her feel happy, alive and excited. She should involve herself in activities that reflect the person she dreams of becoming and only date men who will make her feel proud and not secretly shameful. It will take time for her to build the confidence that she feels worthy of her own good life. However, I am certain that she will continue to work through the barriers to get to her authentic self.

> **TRUST YOUR HEART AND SOUL TO SHOW YOU WHO YOU ARE, THEN FIGHT TO BECOME YOUR AUTHENTIC SELF.**

Chapter 5
At Your Service

A lady who operates very effectively has a servant's spirit. She is also able to function interdependently to achieve her goals and her dreams. Her focus is on becoming who she was born to be; her energy is devoted to those areas that feed her spirit and soul. This woman's influence reaches many shores, and she impacts everyone encountered on her path because she deeply cares for others. These women give their time, talent and treasures to help others; their service is the highest form of humanity.

Meet Lisa Ruffin…

Lisa Ruffin grew up with challenges as a beautiful African American girl. Though she struggled to make friends, Lisa was always self-aware, and knew at eight years old who she wanted to be and what she wanted to do. Though Lisa struggles with perfectionism—becoming frustrated with herself when she does not achieve her ultimate best—she persists to live the life she dreamed. Personal growth is her motto. Every day she looks to learn something new or develop a better way of living. She focuses on paying attention to life.

Not only did Lisa pay attention to life, she created the Little Miss African American (LMAA) Scholarship Pageant—the only pageant of its kind. At the time this book is being written, LMAA is in its 23rd year. LMAA is a nonprofit educational scholarship organization for girls ages six through twelve, and it is designed to give each girl Confidence, Awareness and Pride (CAP).

Following her childhood dreams, Lisa graduated from the Julliard School. She has enjoyed an illustrious career as a Broadway choreographer, and has performed on television as an actress and dancer. Her choreography credits include *The Steve Harvey Show* and UPN's *Moesha*. Lisa is the youngest African American woman to choreograph a Broadway stage production, a show called *Up Close and Personal*.

What makes Lisa extraordinary is that she devotes her talent, resources and energy to ensure that young African American girls are equipped with education, poise, grace and the ability to stand with their heads held high and articulate their dreams and aspirations in front of hundreds of people. Lisa has faithfully fought to provide this opportunity to young African American girls in her pursuit to help build strong, educated, prolific and confident women.

In 2015, several of the former LMAA contestants returned to the pageant to coach the current contestants. These young coaches exemplified poise, grace and confidence. They spoke of being shy and awkward during their younger years and expressed how LMAA met its goal of giving each girl a CAP (Confidence, Awareness and Pride).

Many girls in underserved neighborhoods, who have met with unfortunate circumstances, have benefitted greatly from the LMAA. One area that is particularly important for girls is to be able to speak publicly, which by the way is said to be the No. 1 fear of most people. Imagine the confidence that a young girl gains when she is able to stand before hundreds of people and give a speech she has memorized. This practice will help her speak in the classroom and in the boardroom. Public speaking is only one benefit that the girls receive; the participants meet new friends and build life-long relationships. The skills are vital for students, future leaders, politicians and entrepreneurs.

There is research which finds that girls are far less likely to raise their hands in class than boys, and girls are less likely to participate in politics because they lack the confidence to speak publicly. In their book *The Confidence Code: The Science and Art of Self-Assurance—What Women Should Know,* authors Katty Kay and Claire Shipman write about research on the differences in levels of confidence between men and women. They cite a study conducted at the University of Milan by psychologist Zach Estes. Estes found that the reason women didn't do as well was because they didn't answer some of the questions on a test. When questioned about how confident they were in their answers, the women did not score well. The research of Estes concluded broadly that "the natural result of under-confidence is inaction."

As a former beauty queen, I've experienced the benefits of practicing confidence in pageants. I entered my first pageant, the Our Little Miss pageant, at the age of 14. There were over 500 contestants, only five of whom were African Americans. I think I won Honorable Mention for my talent, but what I took away was more rewarding than the crown. It takes grace, faith and a sense of self to stand in front of people and be judged. Moreover, it takes pride, poise and determination to lose and keep on competing. For me, the journey of self-exploration began at that tender age of 14, a journey to discover who I was and what I had to offer the world. I had always thought that I was a Queen; I only needed to get a crown.

What many people misunderstand about pageants is that you learn more about yourself than you think you'll learn. It's not really about competing with the other contestants, but rather you compete with yourself to be your best self. Throughout your life, your most challenging competitor will be your former self.

Lisa Ruffin epitomizes living love, and she is doing so with passion, pride and a heart to build up her community—one little girl at a time. Lisa's legacy will be the influence she has had on the young girls who struggle with shyness, fear of speaking in public, and fear of performing in front of others. She is helping to build and enforce educational standards that have led many of the girls to attend college and become productive members of society. The lives of so many people are positively impacted when you give young girls the opportunity to be educated in areas of personal growth and healthy competition.

Introducing Janice Kamenir-Reznik...

Another powerful woman who is changing the world is Janice Kamenir-Reznik—a mother, wife, attorney and now activist who retired from her law practice over 12 years ago to establish a nonprofit. One day she was contacted by her rabbi who asked if she would partner with him to start the organization, Jewish World Watch (JWW). JWW was formed to galvanize the Jewish community to "do something" rather than just talk about the issues of genocide affecting Darfur and the Republic of Congo. As Co-founder and President of JWW, Janice embraced the call to action and has not looked back.

She has travelled to these countries on several occasions and spent time with the women and children. At times these trips were very uncomfortable for Janice because she suffers from car sickness and the areas she visited have no paved roads. Could you imagine driving four hours on a desolate road to visit a town with shanty homes, no running water—with the intention to help people who you don't know and who live thousands of miles away from you? And, of course, there is always the risk of danger.

What makes Janice extraordinary is that she has all the comforts of the good life. She is married to a successful attorney, lives in a beautiful home, and enjoys a great life. She is educated and can pretty much write her own ticket. Yet, she uses her life to help others.

JWW has partnered with HEAL Africa and implemented the Safe Motherhood program. Safe Motherhood works with Congolese rape survivors and trains them to sell produce and to work in the fields. They use the proceeds to train birth assistants and pay for surgeries that are needed when women are severely injured as a result of being gang-raped. In Darfur, survivors living in refugee camps are in constant danger of being raped if they leave the refugee camps to get water. To assist the refugees, JWW has implemented the solar cooking project so women can cook food and remain in the camps. Today, 150,000 refugees are using solar cooking.

In the Congo, JWW is also teaching men how to respect girls and women, using a bible-based model program, Sons of Congo, which has helped over 25,000 men. JWW also pays tuition for children to attend school to keep them from falling prey to the militia. The organization was instrumental in building the Chambucha Rape and Crisis Center in the Congo to serve girls and women who have survived rape and violence.

Impacting the World

Do you see yourself in either of these women? In what area can you change and impact the world? There are so many ways we can impact the world and we can start in our own backyards.

Small things matter as much as big things. You can make a difference one little thing at a time. It is a blessing to be able to help others and doing so benefits both the giver and the recipient. Better health, a sense of pride, and a longer life are a few of the significant benefits of helping others. In his book, *Love Leadership: The New Way to Lead in a Fear-Based World*,

John Hope Bryant writes, "Giving inspires loyalty, attracts good people, confers peace of mind, and lies at the core of true wealth."

Years ago, I had the opportunity to do a small favor for a friend who is a producer. Then newly divorced, she had a job offer to work on a project in Africa for two months. When she asked me to take care of her home and children (two boys, ages ten and twelve), I was honored and challenged. I secretly wondered what it would be like to have more than one child. It is the highest form of respect and trust when a woman allows you to care for her children and her home. To be able to give a friend the opportunity of a lifetime was very exciting for me.

When we give to others, we receive more from life. Your giving will nourish you and the receiver. Look for opportunities in life to help others in an area that you are passionate about. What do you care about? What would you do if you could alter the course of someone's life? Each and every day, the decisions we make in our lives give us the opportunity to affect change in the world.

MEASURE YOUR REWARDS IN LIFE BY WHAT YOU GIVE TO OTHERS.

Chapter 6
The Power in a Woman

Power is a blessing and a gift. When you find it, you will realize your reason for living. Long before she hit the campaign trail supporting her husband's campaign for the presidency, Michelle Obama was a Harvard Law School student helping the poor in the areas of landlord-tenant and family law issues. Then as Michelle Robinson, and now as First Lady, Michelle Obama has always sought to make an impact in the world at large.

When a woman makes a choice to live her life to its fullest, she opens the flood gates of opportunities, dreams and desires for other women to seek their power. Using our gifts and talents gives others permission to do so as well. A line in the popular tune "India's Song" by India Arie epitomizes the subconscious feeling at the core of a woman's dreams and desires to be in connection with her soul in her home, her career and in her relationships.

In 2000, on *The Oprah Winfrey Show*, Gary Zukav stated that "Power is the alignment of your personality with your soul." It is your passion that gives you your power. When a woman decides to fully live life with purpose and passion, she will experience her God-given power. God has blessed me with the gifts of dance, understanding, wisdom and a servant's heart. It is through these gifts that I am empowered to do my best and to be my best. These areas are where I am able to allow my light to shine without reservation and without apology. My gifts are also my passions.

They are the things that I care about and the things to which I will give my time, talent and treasure. I can dance for hours and talk with a friend in need for days. Everything that I read is about how to give or to help others. It is obvious to me that my passion is to serve others.

Power from Passion

It is vitally important for your life that you find your passion. Why? Because living your life without your passion is like going to the grocery store and buying food that you don't like and will not cook. You waste your money and your time. What's the point of living life if it's not the one that you were created to live?

Have you ever looked at someone's life and wished that you could have their life? They may travel the world, or have a happy relationship or marriage. Maybe they have lots of friends or participate in fun events, or they have a dream career that you wish you could have. What you really wish is to experience the glow and happiness of living your own life.

Let's talk about the area of career. I believe that certain jobs are meant only to teach us skills in preparation for what God has gifted us to do. If you're not working in the area of your passion, you must use every opportunity in your current position to propel yourself to move closer to the place where you'll find your true passion. Most of us, however, have no clue where our powers lie. Well, your power is in your passions, which are most often found in your natural talent, and that is God's gift to you. You may be able to find success in any area, but your "true" power will be unleashed from finding your passion.

Faced with several tragedies as a teenager, Jacques McNeil found her passion, and because she has, we all will benefit. Jacques is the author of *Life Happens: 30 Strategies for Triumphant Living* and founder of the Women Inspiring Through Network

Elements Sister To Sister (W.I.T.N.E.S.S.) Book Club. This book club also holds a monthly prayer conference. Throughout her book, she shares stories of her life that would have broken the spirit of most of us. Yet through her resilient and faithful spirit, Jacques has become a strong and powerful leader who is revered by her husband and serves as a role model for her daughter. She is a woman who makes other women want to be better and do better, the epitome of "iron sharpening iron."

Born to Dance!

As a young girl growing up in the San Francisco Bay area, it was apparent that I was a gifted dancer. From the time I could walk, I danced. My ability to move fluidly and effortlessly was amazing and everyone could see it. Perhaps there is something about you that everyone can see, but that you cannot. When you recognize it and you nurture it, this can become your power. It's already in you. Your true potential is tied to it.

Throughout the years of my life, I have used my talent and gift of dance to generate a source of income, to teach others, and to recognize my own power. I have been blessed to be able to dance past the age when most dancers hang up their dancing shoes. When I dance, I inspire, I motivate, and I prove to others that their dreams are attainable. When I'm dancing, I enter the zone, a place where I am my true self and my power is set free. I am alive. Through dance, I am empowered to be hopeful, to fight, and to achieve my ideal life, as well as to inspire other women to do the same.

Misty Tripoli…Helping People Find Their Groove

Misty Tripoli, a beautiful, energetic, vibrant sensual woman, is impacting the world through her passion for fitness, dance and music. As a child, she was grossly overweight and insecure.

Her desire to be healthy and happy led her to create "The World Groove Movement." I met Misty in Los Angeles on one of her stops to the West Coast. She constantly travels the world inspiring and instructing women and men on how to let go and connect the body and mind.

I answered a call to participate in a workshop that was showcasing her new style of dance called "Groove." The agreement was that you had to participate for the entire month to gain the benefits and to report your progress. So for one month I got out of bed at 5:00 in the morning to be at the dance studio at 6:00 a.m. to experience Groove for two hours before I went to work.

The idea behind Grooving is to move your body in any way that you want to with the music. There is no choreography, no specific way you should move your body other than what your spirit feels. As a trained dancer who is still in training, I found this technique very difficult because I was expecting to be taught something that I could follow. The thought of moving around for two hours without any direction was very uncomfortable for me. I'm a good dancer but I'm not the best choreographer, so I was very apprehensive.

Grooving was a life-changing experience for me as a person and also as a performer. The idea of allowing my body to decide what it wanted to do was so different for me and most of the students. The hardest part was getting past how I looked if my body wanted to move into a position that was not flattering to me.

As a dancer, everything is about lines. Your movement is always beautiful and makes total sense from the perspective of dance, unless you are Grooving. As you Groove, your body might end up with your butt in the sky and your head between your legs—not pretty at all! However, the method of Grooving is intended to awaken your consciousness through music and movement, and allow yourself to be free from judgment and criticism. Grooving gave me an inner confidence that is unexplainable. It strengthened my body, my soul and freed my mind. And as an added bonus, I lost five pounds.

Misty's method is considered controversial by some and life-changing by others. But what is a fact is that Misty has the power to change the world and she is doing just that. She is helping thousands of people find their "groove" and move their bodies.

Hone in on Your Power

Where is your power? What gives your life meaning and energizes you? It is important that women spend time recognizing and developing their passion. Talk to your family members, friends and people who've known you for years. Spend quiet time with God and listen for your calling. As you begin to hone in on your Power, you will begin to become more authentic and effective. You will begin to operate from a place deep inside your soul when you are driven by your passion. Trust me, if you fail to live your true life, you'll always feel as if something is missing. Your power is real. Your power is alive. Your power exists. Find it and use it.

YOUR NATURAL TALENT IS WHERE YOUR POWER LIES.

Chapter 7
L.O.V.E. and Happiness

Everybody knows somebody who is never happy. No matter what the situation is, these people can find something to fuss, argue or complain about at any time. They are never happy and never content. I'm sure you're not one of these people because you are reading this book, but I know you know a co-worker or friend who has this issue. Let me say that I can understand someone's frustration when things don't go the way they want them to go, and I can go along with Type A behavior as a problem area, but the group that stands under the "Happyness" umbrella is different. [My use of the misspelled version of happiness is to denote the dysfunction in selective happiness - to show how every circumstance and situation should not change your level of happiness. Unfortunately, I have seen good marriages end over the "perception" of "happyness."]

A Flat Tire Mentality

Many people associate happiness with their circumstances. A bad day can consist of losing their cell phone, running out of gas, or missing a nail appointment. Let's call them "circumstantially happy" people. If the circumstances are perfect, then they're happy. If the circumstances are not perfect, then their happiness is compromised.

A former co-worker was this type of person. As long as

everything in her life was perfect, she was happy (in her case, not complaining meant happy). The truth was that she did not know how to be happy regardless of her circumstances.

One day, she had a flat tire on a busy Los Angeles freeway on the way to work. She was upset all day. In her words, how could she be happy when she had a flat tire and had to buy a new tire? Seriously, she was mad and complained *the entire day*. I often wondered what response she would have had to a real major life event. Her normal responses to minor inconveniences were so over-the-top, that I imagine there would be no other alternative but to self-destruct if she had a major negative life event.

What people like her fail to appreciate is that there are so many reasons to be happy and most of them have to do with being grateful. However, you must be content to be grateful and to be content you must be able to sit with whatever situation you find yourself in until it changes.

When my co-worker told me the story about her flat tire, my first thought was "Thank God it was just a flat tire." My second thought was "I'm glad no one crashed into her car when the tire blew out." In my mind, tires would actually be a welcome expense for me, especially considering all the expenses that you can incur when an automobile malfunctions on a busy Los Angeles freeway. If you really thought about it, a flat tire would be cause to jump and shout for joy, not become depressed for an entire day.

Happiness & Spirituality

Authors Baker and Stauth, in their book *What Happy People Know*, contend that neither love, career nor money will bring happiness. But a lack of spiritual awareness will ensure unhappiness. Throughout their book, there are numerous stories of men and women who suffered unimaginable tragedies, yet were happier than those people whose lives should have been happy but were not. I believe that our purpose is to share spiritual qualities with all women and to remind them and ourselves that happiness is an inside job.

A renowned radio talk show psychologist made a statement that 90% of all people who commit suicide have no spiritual or religious affiliation. It made sense to me. Without God or some other higher power to connect to, life would be too scary and at times unbearable. The search for happiness would be futile. Happiness is an integral part of spirituality.

Happiness in Relationship/Marriage

For those of you who want to be married, if you can acknowledge that you may have a tendency to stand under the "happyness" umbrella, then you are in a good position to have a satisfying marriage. Happiness is subjective because it is dependent upon our ability to recognize the difference between our perspective and the truth. Some people give the appearance that they are never satisfied, even though there is nothing necessarily wrong. Small matters, like not turning off the lights when leaving the house, neglecting to take out the trash, or not picking up behind oneself can create unhappyness in a home that is otherwise happy.

Most of us recognize and know that idiosyncrasies are just minor irritants. What we don't understand is that left unchecked, they turn into deal breakers without us even realizing it. For example, when we are choosing a man that we want to be our "one and only" love of our life, we may overlook idiosyncrasies. Later, we might look back and see that a minor irritant that seemed cute at one time was really something that we could not and would not live with.

One of my clients was attracted to men who were either actors or musicians. Their creativity and sensitivity made her feel comfortable, and she believed that an artist's sensitivity would translate into quiet arguments, and easy evenings at home. Unfortunately, she missed one very important part of the creative lifestyle—the fact that because of the creative and sporadic nature of acting and musicianship, there would be many times when she would have to be alone and other times when she would be responsible for the finances.

Happiness Is a State of Mind

Smart women know that being happy is a choice. Happiness is a spiritual issue. Many people attach happiness to situations, when in essence it is a state of mind that has nothing to do with what's going on in your life.

A HAPPY LIFE IS A CHOICE.

Chapter 8
If The Gift Fits, Wear It

Everyone reading this book has been bestowed with multiple gifts. You may not yet be aware of what those gifts are, but I can assure you that they exist. Most of the women being highlighted in this book are not celebrities, but they should be celebrated for their commitment to family, their community and the world at large.

So many of you are worthy of praise for the things that you contribute to society, and I want to honor you in that way. With that said, one celebrity comes to my mind as a woman who is living in her gifting to the world—Oprah. This woman is my muse and my mentor. Her ability to touch, attract, inspire, entice and charm people to action is unmatched. If you really think about it, she got rich by giving opportunity to others. And, as we all know, everything she touched related to others turned to gold. Like Oprah, my passion in life is to help you find your gifting and to live your life and leave your legacy.

What Is Your Legacy?

Have you actually thought about the legacy that you want to leave of your existence on the planet? How do you want to be remembered? What gifts do you want people to talk about at your home-going service (i.e., funeral)? Do you want to be remembered as the party girl who was at every celebration? Or as the woman who impacted the lives of others through her philanthropy?

Many women play down their gifts while emotionally crying out for someone to help develop and expose them. We have come a long way but we can be still a bit ashamed of our ambitions. There seems to be a chip in the female brain that goes on the blink whenever we get close to our life goals and dreams. It automatically plays down any major success that we might achieve.

As an effective woman, you have a commitment to nurture, expose and share all of your gifts and talents with others. It is your birthright. The Bible admonishes us to "Let our light shine." Are you sure whether or not you are letting your light shine? For instance, have you ever wondered why God gifted some people with the talent of cooking—I mean the kind of cooking that doesn't require a recipe and they can prepare a gourmet meal in less than 30 minutes? We all know someone like this. I envy them!

My friend, Dawn, is such a person. Not only is she an educational consultant, great mother and wife, but when she comes into a kitchen you can hear string instruments playing melodic sounds announcing the Queen of the Kitchen has arrived. She chops her veggies perfectly, makes scones (who does that?), and prepares her own sauces. *Really?* This is truly her gifting. It is also her passion. She enjoys talking about food, reading about food, and preparing the meals. Dawn shines when she is working with food.

More Examples

Another girlfriend, Iyanna, a former dancer and now prolific trainer, can make you do things with your body that you didn't know were possible. Training and studying with her is like learning to paint from Picasso. I trained with her on the Pilates reformer machine a few times and my core had never been worked out in that way. For an entire week, I couldn't get my stomach to protrude. It was physically impossible (every woman's dream). Her attention to detail and ability to get amazing results is why her clients continue to show up year after year.

What about the woman who can single-handedly raise a family of six children and put them all through college, or the woman who has a talent for creating beauty out of nothing, or the woman who has the ability to give to others and still remain smiling and unjaded?

My sister is gifted with the ability to decorate. Her homes have always looked like they were designed and featured in Better Homes and Gardens magazine. She can mix fabrics and patterns in a way that is baffling to most of us. The level of skill that she possesses as an interior designer is equivalent to the Home & Garden Television (HGTV) design staff, and she did not learn it in school.

Have Too Many Gifts?

There are those who are so gifted that they have questions like "I have too many gifts…which gift should I use?" That's a good question, and one to which I don't have an answer. I also feel that God blessed me with an abundance of talents. I have struggled all my life to find out how to use what I've been given.

However, there is one very gifted woman who is navigating her way through her many gifts with grace and ease. Angelique Talbert, wife and mother of one son and two daughters, is a Mary Kay sales director and founder of Sparkle Girls. Angelique is a bubbly, vibrant and spirited woman. Through her Sparkle Girls organization, she mentors and encourages young girls to find their passion and purpose and to operate from their essence.

It is important to her that these girls gain self-confidence, self-esteem and presence. As a Mary Kay sales director, she continues to inspire passion and purpose in so many women as she helps them build their businesses, while providing a venue for them to collaborate and to grow. Armed with a degree in marketing, she masterfully turns a small project into a piece of art. Angelique's vision and pioneering spirit coupled with a heart to serve her community is truly a gift.

Use Your Gifts Daily

The best advice that I can offer is to incorporate your gifts into your daily life (all of them) and to share with others the ones that you are most passionate about. A place to start to determine your special gift is to ask people who are close to you. What compliments do you repeatedly receive? For example, do you always receive compliments on your style of dress? Or how you apply your makeup or your ability to articulate complicated ideas? Are you good at resolving conflict? Chances are others have been trying to tell you where you are gifted for years. But you didn't hear them because your gifts came naturally to you.

Looking back over my own life, I have been dancing, writing and coaching people since I was in junior high school. I remember writing love letters and break-up letters for my friends, and unsent letters to boys expressing my hurt and pain over break-ups. Everyone came to me for advice on what to do when they were confused. I had an answer for everything. Similarly, since I could walk, I have danced and people have told me all of my life that I was an excellent dancer. Although my passion and my gift of dance did not become my main career, I did not abandon my gift.

However we determine our gifts, they are a vital part of our ability to live a full and happy life. Of course, we can "make do" but to be totally and completely satisfied with life we must find and develop our natural gifts.

> **NEVER DENY WHO YOU ARE TO BECOME SOMEONE YOU'RE NOT. YOU WILL HAVE TO FIGHT TO GET BACK TO THE PERSON GOD MADE YOU.**

Chapter 9
Money Matters

There are some people who have a natural talent for spending money wisely, living within their means, and saving for the proverbial "rainy day." And then there are the 80% who are clueless. That's not a research statistic, but an educated guess. We constantly struggle to make ends meet and live from paycheck to our next payday advance. We can't even make it to payday anymore. What we never learned is that "money matters"—but not the way we have been programmed to believe.

Dealing with money requires discipline, knowledge and a desire to learn. In her book, *Rich Woman,* Kim Kiyosaki shares information on various types of investments. Kim is the wife of best-selling author Robert Kiyosaki (*Rich Dad, Poor Dad*), and she is not sitting on her laurels while her husband lives his dream life. She is building her own life and legacy. Her book is a wealth of information for a woman who is serious about her financial freedom.

Changing Times

Life has changed since our parents were young. Women are no longer waiting for a husband to take care of them. And it's a good thing because men are not marrying as young as they did in the past. Consequently, they are not necessarily willing to take on the weight of being the sole breadwinner in the family.

Also, many men are not financially savvy or capable of handling money in a disciplined manner, nor do they desire to take on that responsibility.

Times have changed and so must we. Along with our health and spiritual life, a woman must keep her financial house in order. We need to live within our financial means while planning for our future. Of course, having a husband who can handle all of your financial responsibilities is a blessing. Yet we should understand that as an individual we had better maintain our own FICO credit score and be able to support our husbands if the need arises. The wedding vows state, "For better, for worse, for richer, for poorer, in sickness and in health…"

In the old days, men worked and handled all of the money and paid the bills. When the husband died, the wife didn't have any knowledge or skill to financially care for herself. As a result, the wife was left to the mercy of other people to manage her life and money. Times have changed, but you must take advantage of the changes if you don't want to end up in the same situation.

What Did You Learn about Money?

It's amazing to me that in 2016, if asked, many people still believe that old axiom that money will make you happy and will solve all of your problems. Even though we have numerous examples of "rich" people who dispel this myth, those of us whose bank accounts are anorexic will swear that if we had the money of stars like Ariana Grande or Beyoncé, our lives would be better.

What we have not learned about money is that it is about financial freedom, and financial freedom does not give you freedom from your emotional problems, marital woes or mental issues. As a matter of fact, according to Suze Orman, financial freedom begins in your mind, with your thoughts. Suze says that all understanding and thoughts about money are directly tied to our early formative years of experience with money.

In essence, we learn how we feel about money from our experiences with our parents. My early experience with money was watching my single mother work three jobs to take care of her four children. She owned her home and only purchased expensive quality clothing and furniture. She was very mindful to insure everything she purchased.

One situation that stands out in my mind is back-to-school shopping. I only got enough new clothes for the first week of school. Other girls wore new clothes the first two weeks of school. My mother bought fewer items but they were classic pieces. Of course, like many teenagers, my focus was on quantity, not quality.

Orman also says that "Money messages are passed down from generation to generation." The money message that I received as a child was to save your money, buy quality over quantity, purchase items that are classic because they are timeless and you get more bang for your buck. It's a good idea to spend some time thinking about how you were influenced or shamed about money during your past. It can help you teach better money principles to your children.

Sticking to Your Budget or Buying in Excess?

In his book, *God's Leading Lady*, the world-renowned preacher T.D. Jakes writes, "A leading lady is secure enough to stick to a budget, smart enough to budget, and wise enough to stick with the budget once it's in place."

I can hear you thinking, "What's a budget and where can I buy one?" Women spend an enormous amount of money. The problem is that we spend money we don't have on things that we don't need. If women spent half the money they spend thoughtlessly on building a business and preparing for the future, we wouldn't need as much stuff. Owning and operating a business is not only sexy, it's also empowering. It gives you a glow that cosmetics can't give you, while keeping the flow of cash coming in.

Dr. Portia Jackson is a lady operating very effectively in the area of finance. She has masterfully learned to use her knowledge of finances and her discipline to create wealth and opportunity for her family. I first met Portia in a class that she taught on finances. A few years after that, she started a podcast show, *Working Motherhood*, that highlights the successes and struggles of working mothers. The show is informative, engaging and inspiring. I love listening to the women share their victories, most of which are born out of struggles and challenges.

Money should be used as a tool to give your life meaning and to allow you to live your soul's desire. Use your money to learn new things, help others, and to build a legacy for your children's children. Money used only to buy excess "stuff" is not a good use of money. Really, ladies! Just how many pairs of black shoes do you need? Don't answer that!

Our desire for excess has literally made our lives miserable. The fall of the housing market is just one result of our excessiveness. Someone once said, "Just because an item is on sale, doesn't mean you can afford it."

Money as Financial Freedom

As a marriage mentor, I have seen good marriages devastated because money issues have created certain dynamics that caused each individual to come face-to-face with his or her Money Self. (Your Money Self is how you feel about money, use money, and how you respond to life when you are living beyond your means.) I have also seen relationships and successful marriages in which each partner embraces his or her Money Self, and money can then be used as a tool for achieving financial freedom.

What is financial freedom? I'm still learning and working toward it. My understanding of financial freedom is that it allows you the opportunity to live in the way that you desire. Having said that, let me clarify something for those of you who may be battling with blind spots.

Money can pay your doctors, but it can't make you well. Money can buy you things, but the things you buy won't love you back. Money will give you peace of mind only if you handle the other areas in your life that can destroy your peace.

NOTE TO MARRIED WOMEN

Your ability to communicate effectively with your husband will be more important than the amount of money that you have available to you. The lack of money does not make or break your marriage. Instead, a lack of desire to work through relational, financial and communication problems, an inability to compromise, and the need to place blame can be more responsible for the demise of a relationship than the lack of money.

FINANCIAL FREEDOM IS NOT THE ANSWER TO EVERY PROBLEM—ONLY FINANCIAL PROBLEMS.

Chapter 10
L.O.V.E. and Fear are Enemies

When we are afraid to follow our hearts, we run the risk of living our entire lives in discontent. It is so easy for many of us to just exist. We go through the motions of our days believing that we are living an authentic life. Then one day we realize that it is our representative (false self) that is actually running things. Our representative is the self that shows up to the interview when we're looking for a new job. It is also our representative that shows us in our best light upon meeting a new friend. Our representative would never show a new date what type of person we really are. As a matter of fact, the representative won't allow us to be a best friend, a great parent, or a true partner in a relationship. Why is that? Because the representative is not real. It is a persona that is developed to keep us from being afraid. And the one thing that we must do to reach our pinnacle of success in any area of our life is to overcome our fear.

Growing Tired of Fear

For most of my young adult life, I struggled with fear. I was afraid to make decisions, afraid not to make decisions, afraid of dying, afraid of living too well, afraid of loving, and afraid of not being loved. My obsessive thoughts of fear stemmed from a childhood that was riddled with fear messages from a single parent whose primary goal was to protect her children from harm.

The culture during my mother's own childhood was one that believed a child should be fearful of the parent in order to keep the child from misbehaving. Some feel this is the residue left over from slavery, and it makes sense to me. The slave master made sure that the slaves were afraid to misbehave and therefore he had control over them. I'm not sure whether this approach worked in other families, but it surely didn't work in mine, nor did it work for some slaves. They escaped when they were tired of be held captive. Their desire to be free was stronger than their fear of the master.

Both my younger brother and I misbehaved, and even so, my childhood left me with a fearful mindset that took many years to resolve. During those years, I read everything I could get my hands on relating to fear and courage, starting with my Bible. By the time I reached the age of 30, I was fed up with fear and ready to stop the insanity that was allowing my past to ruin my future. It was time to change the paradigm of my life.

Fear's Cast of Characters

One of the books that helped me let go of fear was *Hinds Feet on High Places* written by Hannah Hurnard. The book is an allegory depicting the life journey we must travel if we are to live in "high places." High places represent principles of living.

This story was instrumental in reminding me what being a child of God really means and how my faith, not my works, would eliminate my fear. The character Much-Afraid lived in the village of Much Trembling. Her family, the Fearings, wanted Much-Afraid to marry Craven-Fear.

Much-Afraid had been raised by an aunt, Mrs. Dismal Foreboding, along with her cousins, Gloomy, Spiteful, and Craven-Fear, the family bully. Eventually, Much-Afraid took a risk and ran away from the village of Much Trembling and traveled to the high places with her companions, Sorrow and Suffering. With hard work, she was able to overcome her many fears. Much-Afraid took a risk to become what she knew she could become.

Does this story remind you of anyone? Much-Afraid's story is the story of so many women. This cast of characters fills our homes and lives. It is the new parent who attempts to protect the child from danger by picking him up from school, just two blocks away from home. Instead, she might consider teaching the child to take a safe route, call home in case of trouble, and walk with a friend. It's the woman over 40 who wants to return to school to obtain a college degree but is afraid that she is too old to compete with the younger college-aged students. It's the young girl who has always dreamed of backpacking across Europe but has allowed fear messages from others to prevent her from achieving this lifelong dream.

Do you live in the village of Much-Trembling? Don't feel bad if you live there. The good news is that, as long as you know where you are, you can change. Think about it. Do you feel reluctant to move forward with an idea or goal? Is fear holding you back from changing jobs, finding a husband, going to school, writing a screenplay or book, traveling to a remote country, or becoming an entrepreneur?

Fear & Your Past

Do you know anyone who is paralyzed by fear because of how they were raised? Of course you do, we all do. The impact of the way we grew up has a powerful influence on how we respond to life. If you grew up in a family where you received fear messages, you learned fear. If you grew up receiving opportunity messages, you learned to seek opportunity. If you grew up in a family where you received fight messages, you learned to fight. When you have been subjected to living within a negative fearful environment, you must fight to keep your dreams alive. Recognize and address those areas where fear and other negative emotions can paralyze your progress.

So now we dive into the deep end of the pool (an analogy used by my pastor to denote that the teaching is going to get more difficult and hard to receive). Being spiritual women, we must exercise the confidence to rely on a higher power to handle the matters that cause us fear.

What Are You Afraid Of?

My goal in writing this book is to help as many women as I can to recognize their passion and their purpose and help them be as successful as possible. To be successful, we must get comfortable with the other side of the coin (failure), while we give all that we have to our goals and dreams.

Do you fear what others will say about you? Success always comes with some envy, jealousy and scrutiny about you, especially if you're in a creative field. Every actress, singer, artist or dancer is subjected to the opinions of their audience and the critics. What you should realize is that whether or not you succeed people will always have an opinion and you will never please everyone.

Are you afraid to move out of one career into a new one? If so, you must realize that you should feel a certain amount of fear when you move into unchartered waters. Do your research, do your work, prepare yourself to move. When you have thoroughly prepared, you will feel less fear. Of course, the uncertainty will linger, but it will subside as you walk in your new position.

Learning to fail well will move you closer to success when you realize that failure is a prerequisite to success. Study successful people and you will begin to see a pattern emerge that will help you be more comfortable as you find your true career choice.

Developing Faith & Trust

One of my favorite authors, Debbie Ford (*The Dark Side of the Light Chasers*), wrote, "...it's nearly impossible to achieve our highest vision for our lives as long as we are guided by our fears." My own life has reflected this truth. Learning to let go of fear and rely on Faith is a strategy that will serve you well. Trusting that the universe is guiding you to make the right choices and decisions will enable you to let go of fear.

START WITH EXPLORING HIDDEN FEARS TO BEGIN YOUR JOURNEY TO SUCCESS.

Chapter 11
Wisdom Is A Gift

Wise people have always intrigued me. They are intelligent, balanced, prudent and tactful. A willingness to receive instruction, make good decisions, and always seek knowledge is the hallmark of a wise one. However, the quality that most attracts me to them is their peacefulness. They have a confidence that others do not have.

Wise or Foolish?

How do we acquire wisdom? How can wisdom help us create the lives that we want? We all have access to knowledge and wisdom. Yet we don't always seek out that access.

Because many of you reading this book are probably women, I will use an example related to a favorite topic for most of us—relationships. When we are out of alignment with our authenticity and in need of love and companionship, we may throw away any semblance of wisdom that we have gained to enter into relationships too quickly, and choose partners who harm us or put us in harm's way. We can give more than we should give, based on the value we perceive in the relationship. And when we have not grown in wisdom, we can fail to take responsibility for our lack of wisdom in these situations.

When I was a teenager, I can remember making some of the dumbest choices in dating. For example, I dated a drug dealer who sold heroin and was over 18 years old (and I didn't even use drugs). I told myself that all people need love and that he was just like any other man. I reasoned that I knew his grandmother and he came from a good family and that he was raised in a Christian home. This obviously was not one of my wisest decisions. Thankfully, the relationship did not last too long and I did not end up in jail for associating with a drug dealer.

My "Maya Angelou"

As life would have it, God sent me an angel to guide me. When I was 18 years old, I met Lakiba Pittman, one of the most talented, creative and wise women that I have ever met. The woman that I am today is because of her teaching and influence. Her beautiful spirit and understanding were refreshing yet confusing for an 18-year-old. But as the years passed and I listened and learned, it became apparent that I was sitting by a woman who was like none other.

Lakiba was a poet, singer, artist, and wife and mother during my formative years. As I watched her navigate through life's harsh terrain, I learned how to use every adversity to my benefit. I can remember sitting on her porch and discussing so many things. She was gracious and honest, compassionate and authentic. The more I think about who she is, the more I am reminded of the impact she made upon me.

Today, Lakiba continues to impart her wisdom through her book, *Bread Crumbs from the Soul*, her art, her spiritual/life coaching, her family and her community work.

Many of us have memories of our unwise decisions and poor choices tucked away within our journals. It's very important for us to have a role model or mentor who can see us and who can influence and impart wisdom to us. Oprah says that everyone should have a Maya Angelou. Maya is to Oprah what Lakiba is to me. These women knew how to live life using their gifts as their guide, and Oprah and I were there to take this wisdom in. They knew the answers to our questions. That wisdom will always guide you to what you need and it can remove you from a bad place where you may have found yourself.

Forgetting Common Sense

One unwise decision that can wreak havoc in a woman's life is dating a married man. I have seen and read about countless women who chose to rationalize the behavior of a cheating man, only to end up in pain. Yet the disappointing outcome can appear clear to an observer of such a relationship.

In 2004, Greg Behrendt and Liz Tuccillo wrote a New York Times best-seller that also became a movie under the same title, *He's Just Not That Into You*. I read the book and saw the movie. They both were embarrassingly revealing about how women approach relationships and how we neglect to use prudent common sense in this area of our lives. The book was hilarious and sad. It seems almost natural to understand that a man who does not pursue you is not into you, at least until he shows that you are more important than some basic everyday behaviors such as spending time with his friends, watching television alone at home, or attending any event alone. Still, so many women can ignore such clues of a man's disinterest.

Women seek wisdom's call because we know its value in our lives. Meanwhile, there are some famous women who are known for "unwise" decisions. I'm not talking about minor mistakes, but choices and decisions that are bad no matter which way you look at them. Eve ate from the tree of life when she was told specifically not to eat from that tree. Monica Lewinsky, a White House intern during the Bill Clinton's presidency, had sexual relations with the married President of the United States.

I know you may be thinking that Bill Clinton was just as responsible as Monica Lewinsky in their huge screw-up, but one component of wisdom is to focus on what you can control—so let's just focus on us as women. Eve listened to a serpent when she knew what God had commanded. She gave over her wisdom to the serpent. She was insecure in what she knew to be true and did not trust her own judgment. Monica should have known that when their relationship went public, she would be humiliated and degraded and that her life would be discredited. Or maybe, like me at 16 years old, she believed in her early twenties that she would not be impacted when and if their indiscretion became known. Unfortunately, for Monica, her lack of wisdom hurt many people and she ended up in shame and embarrassment. This situation led to her go underground for nearly a decade. It's unfortunate that she did not have a wise friend who could have shared some gentle and loving wisdom with her before she ruined her life and her career before it even got started.

For the young ladies reading this book, I offer these stories to you so that you can observe the devastation of a bad choice without having to actually experience it. I have never believed that I could not learn from someone else's mistake. Some will tell you that you should learn your lessons first-hand, but to that I say, Do you have to set your own house on fire to know that fire burns?

Learning from Relationships

Being a part of a sisterhood that fosters accountability, trust and honesty is helpful for women to learn to trust their own voices. Your real friends will tell you the truth. They are willing to risk your relationship for you to know the truth about yourself.

All close relationships are like mirrors—they reflect what and who you are. Wisdom says that if you're constantly attracting and dating men who are non-committal, then there is a part of you that does not want to be committed. If you're consistently ending relationships, there is something about you that either does not want to be close or you lack the necessary understanding to maintain closeness. You may not agree, but sometimes behavior is louder than justifying words.

Final Thoughts on Behaving Wisely

As in love and relationships, using wisdom to guide your life in the direction of your dreams and goals is the hallmark of a smart woman. Former ESPN host and now co-anchor of Good Morning America, Robin Roberts, chose a part-time job as a sports anchor after graduating from college earning only $5.50 per hour over a full-time news anchor/reporter position with a major station WLOX in Biloxi, Mississippi. She knew that her passion for sports would gain her more leverage than chasing a title or money. Everyone was puzzled by her decision to pass up a larger salary and prestigious job opportunity, but Robin knew her passion and followed her heart to everything she wanted and more than she expected.

Seeking wise counsel and using your common sense will take you much farther in life. I've heard people say that "common sense isn't common." Now that you know this, you can prepare yourself to become a wise woman by looking for other women who exercise wisdom in their lives. One of the smartest decisions that you can make is to ask for input when you are not sure and to ask someone who knows more than you. Some of the smartest people in the world are successful because they have learned to put people in place to help them—people who have more knowledge than they have in certain areas.

THE WISE WILL FLY HIGHER.

Chapter 12
Getting Comfortable With Confrontation

Learning to be comfortable with confrontation is one of my own most treasured gifts in life. The day that I began the work to eradicate my discomfort with confrontation was the day that my life changed in every area. I grew up with a rageaholic. My mother's response to any form of conflict was to curse and scream. She stood 5'11" and her dictatorial type of parenting was very intimidating. She did not have discussions or parent/child conversations about our behavior and the impact that it could have on our lives. Like many parents, she just yelled, screamed and punished.

By the time I was a young adult , I had decided never to argue or become angry with anyone. I wanted to avoid any form of disagreement for fear that someone would hurt my feelings and scream at me. I had developed a fear of conflict, and I could not confront anyone about anything.

Interestingly, anyone who has known me since I was about 25 years old will swear that the previous statement is a bold-face lie. What they don't realize is that I learned to confront people and to deal with conflict very well. My experience at home made me believe that disagreements and problems were to be addressed by anger and yelling. It took me years to learn that it's natural to have disagreements and the way to resolve them did not have to be combative.

The Ins and Outs of Confrontation

Do you struggle with handling confrontation? Are you passive in addressing problems and issues?

First, know that confrontation does not have to be negative. Women must understand the importance of communication and the need for confrontation. When you avoid confrontation, you will essentially have to live in a state of denial. Also, you are giving up your power to affect change in your life and are becoming a victim of circumstances if you choose not to address problems. This could be anything from your mother-in-law causing issues in your marriage, or the bad grades your children are getting in school, to the landlord's lack of care for the property that you're renting.

Don't think that these issues will change without your growth in the area of honest reflection and in learning to confront, because they will not. In her book, *Managing Conflict God's Way*, Deborah Smith Pegues says, "We must therefore abandon any negative, preconceived ideas about confrontation and look at the true definition of the word. The prefix 'con' means together or with, and the root 'fron' means to stand to meet face-to-face. Confrontation is simply the act of coming together face-to-face to resolve an issue."

Many women would rather die a slow death than to initiate a conversation where they must express displeasure or address a problem without anger or rage. Realize that being able to express yourself openly and honestly is a quality that will gain you respect from others and, more importantly, you will be able to do it without the need for drama and excessive anger. If you have trouble setting boundaries, it will be difficult, but not impossible, for you to confront someone.

The most misleading notion about confrontation is that you must be angry to confront someone. Actually, if used properly, confrontation can prevent blow-ups, unresolved anger and arguments. Simply being able to express yourself and ask for what you want is confrontation. Asking your boss for a raise is confrontation; discussing your final grade with your professor is confrontation.

There are other situations where you'll need to use this skill to resolve negative situations and hopefully to your benefit—such as when you need to discuss a problem with your significant other, your boss or your neighbor. It really is a skill to be able to approach someone under a stressful circumstance and be able to work out a win-win solution.

Lessons Learned

By the age of 18, I was beginning to feel the effects of my fear to confront. I have always been very intuitive, and because I was afraid of conflict and confrontation, this caused me to be very anxious. I was employed as a legal secretary in a small legal/accounting firm run by Scott O'Brien and Steve Kroff. Scott was easy-going, soft-spoken, and a warm and gentle man. Steve was tough, loud and mean. He had a hard shell, but was soft inside.

Whenever I made a mistake, Steve would scream and yell. Scott, on the other hand, would quietly reprimand me and express his displeasure. Both of their responses caused me great pain because of my inability to confront and to be confronted. My feelings were hurt when Steve got mad, and when Scott got upset I felt tremendous guilt.

What I learned from these situations is that when you're willing to face yourself concerning your own behavior, there is little room for feeling sorry for yourself or guilty. Similarly, when you're able to gently confront others about their behaviors, you will not only gain their respect, but you will also respect yourself. If you're sincere when you question someone, you will usually get clarity as to why they acted in a particular manner.

Other Things You Need to Know

Of course, there is a time to confront and a time to retreat from confrontation. In his classic book, *The Road Less Traveled*, M. Scott Peck writes:

> *To fail to confront when confrontation is required for the nurture of spiritual growth represents a failure to love equally as does thoughtless criticism or condemnation and other forms of active deprivation of caring. If they love their children, parents must, sparingly and carefully perhaps but nonetheless actively, confront and criticize them from time to time, just as they must allow their children to confront and criticize themselves in turn.*

Friendships and relationships that have no conflict are usually superficial and void of true intimacy. The couple that professes that they never argue probably consists of two people who are not talking to each other honestly in the first place. They're likely choosing to avoid issues that will uncover conflict.

Before you confront anyone, you should determine what result you're seeking. Do you want to change a behavior? Are you trying to teach a lesson or reprimand your partner for perceived bad behavior? Maybe you want to set boundaries. Whatever your goal, look for the best way to motivate the listener to hear what you're saying, and speak in a manner that the listener will understand. Be concerned more about the message and the receiver than you are about your need to confront. Use stories or parables to express yourself. Speak from a place that expresses your sincere desire to find an amicable resolution for everyone. Ask for what you want—a better relationship. Then express what you will and will not tolerate.

And lastly, remember to treat others in the same manner that you would like to be treated.

> **FACE IT, CONFRONT IT, AND FIX IT.**

Chapter 13

Your Vision Leads To Your Destiny

Everyone make plans. Whether those plans are conscious or unconscious, spoken or unspoken, written or unwritten, those plans set in motion your action or inaction, which, in turn, determines your entire life.

I don't know who said, "If you fail to plan, you plan to fail," but this maxim has been very true in my own life. It may contain the answers to your most important questions, and it possibly can change your life forever.

Put It in Writing

Oprah Winfrey stated in an article that she never planned to be as successful as she has become. I disagree with her. She has commented many times about looking back through her journals and finding goals, dreams and desires that were written years before, many of which she did not remember writing. The dreams and goals that she wrote in her journal were the seeds she planted that germinated to create the woman we now know as Oprah.

Writing down your goals and dreams is a form of planning. It is laying the foundation for your actions to follow your thinking. It takes the same skill and planning to write a book as it does to run a major corporation. And most of the planning is done in your mind, even before you write 50 pages of your book or begin the business.

The Power of Your Thoughts

Are you aware that your behavior is based on your thoughts? We literally have "thought" ourselves to where we now are in our lives. The little girl who says, "When I grow up, I want to be a mommy," but does not mention being a wife is thinking herself into being a single parent. The little girl who wants to get married and have a family is thinking herself into a family situation.

Here's the caveat with our thinking: sometimes we will have a thought or a dream, but we also have an unconscious underlying belief that is in direct conflict with it. For instance, if you have a goal of becoming a doctor, but you believe in your heart that women don't make good doctors, then your belief has the potential to negatively influence whether you will pursue this goal.

The 4 Aspects of Planning

Have you learned how to plan? Has a lack of planning been a problem? Planning is one of the most important aspects of achieving any objective. A daily list of things to do will give you an idea of what needs to be done on any given day. Another advantage of list-making is that you complete more than you would have without a list.

But there's more! There are actually four aspects to planning: vision, faith, plan and execute.

1. **Vision:** Focus your mind. Be very careful about what you focus on. Visualize where you're going, not where you are.

2. **Faith:** When you want to give up because you've lost sight of your vision, your faith can sustain you.

3. **Plan:** Go back to your vision for your end result. Set a specific action plan in place for the short-term period and the long-term.

4. **Execute:** Start where you are and work toward the goal. Once you begin, you will get help along the way. People and things that you need will find their way to you. Your job is to keep working, even when you don't feel like it or can't see your goal. Trust the process.

It has been said that "a ship without a sail will end up in any port." Similarly, a boat that has a navigational system can get off track, but it will still reach its destination. When we set specific plans in motion, we are more likely to achieve them.

Additional Tips

As a wife, mother, professional dancer, legal assistant, author, entrepreneur, fitness trainer, motivational speaker, former beauty queen, model, life coach and college graduate, the life that I live today is a direct result of my childhood visions. I saw myself living each of these goals, and the proof is written on the pages of the journals from my youth. As in the case of Oprah, there is power in the words that grace our journals.

Once you commit a thought to paper, you set the wheels in motion to achieve any goal or dream. Someone said, "Until a goal is written down and has a date attached to it, it is just a dream." The difference between a goal and a dream is that a goal has a specific date attached to it. A dream can become a goal if it is specific and measurable.

I recommend that everyone write an "I Have a Dream" speech. Dr. Martin Luther King Jr.'s famous speech still brings tears to my eyes. As a young girl, I fell in love with Dr. King. He embodied the internal qualities that I admired; his courage, his faith and his ability to fight for what he believed in were inspiring to me.

This year I recorded my first "I have a dream" speech and

listening to it brought tears to my eyes when I heard it. Why? Because my speech exemplified the goals of the little girl who dreamed in Technicolor and whose dreams were unencumbered by fears and "what ifs." I believe in the words of Napoleon Hill, "Whatever your mind can conceive and believe, it can achieve."

Some of you may be saying, I hate lists and I don't want to keep track of my every thought or dream that I have. Well, maybe you might consider making a vision board. Collect photos of places you want to visit, goals you want to achieve, or cars you might want to drive. The idea is to give your mind a visual focus.

The Power of Books, Theater & Film

In 2013, my husband was hired to direct a play titled *Things That Make Men Cry* written by a beautiful woman, Dr. Gloria Morrow. Dr. Morrow is a visionary with a passion for women's issues. From the moment that I met her, I knew that we would be friends. She exuded the grace of an African queen, the kindness of a loving mother, and her love of helping others poured from her spirit.

With the success of her books, Dr. Morrow has a vision of reaching larger groups of people, and because of her artistic talent, it was a natural progression for her to begin writing plays. In 2015, her stage play *Three Times a Lady* opened. It was a thought-provoking, emotion-stirring journey. It was a story of a woman whose husband came home one day and asked for a divorce. The play shows the woman's meltdown and eventual growth as she addresses issues of the past that prevented her from having a better marriage and happier life. It shows how she found her way back to her true self through therapy and self-reflection.

Dr. Morrow is currently working on her next play. She is impacting both men and women through her literary and theatrical works. On that note, books and movies have long had the power to change and impact lives. In my own life, I have been moved to action because I read a particular book or saw a movie that inspired me to change my behavior or to become a better human being. As you embrace the vision of your future, remember to keep your eyes on the prize no matter what the road looks like.

> **WHAT YOU FOCUS ON WILL GUIDE THE DIRECTION THAT YOUR LIFE WILL TAKE. MAKE SURE YOUR VISION IS AIMED AT YOUR PURPOSE.**

Chapter 14

Watch Your Mindset

Where you are in life today is a direct result of the thoughts that you have allowed to manifest. The decisions you have made or not made have landed you right where you are. If I had a dollar for every time I have heard someone say the previous two sentences, I would be a very rich woman.

Hopefully you are positioned exactly where you want to be. If not, now is the time to change directions and to begin thinking thoughts that will move you to where you want to go. As long as you are alive, you have the opportunity to turn your life around at any point you decide to change your mindset.

Dangerous Directions

It should be a comfort to know that everything that happens in life allows you the opportunity to refocus and readjust. So no matter where you are, it is where you are supposed to be for now. Where you are is just temporary, sort of like a layover at an airport on a trip to your final destination.

When you're on a layover between flights, it can be for a short or long period of time. If it's the airline's fault, some companies will give you accommodations, while others let you figure out the details of your layover. These events are sometimes unexpected and uncomfortable, and the severity of your experience of the layover will depend on how you choose to handle the situation.

Karen (not her real name), a woman of retirement age, was laid off from her job of over 10 years. Immediately after being laid off, she went out looking for work and met with rejection at every turn. Feeling painfully rejected and without any desire to look objectively at her situation, she allowed her mind to create a dangerous lifestyle. I learned from a friend who is a world-renowned psychologist that this is called Situational Depression.

Karen became depressed, and in a short period of time, her thinking caused her to become careless. One day, she fell and hurt her knees. Then she had a freak accident where she was dragged by her friend's car. Her mind was creating emotional chaos, which was causing her to be careless and not mindful of her actions. During this time, Karen also cut herself off from her close friends, stopped exercising, and spent most of her time watching television. She fell into an abyss of self-focus and unrecognized depression.

If we look back over our life, we can all remember a time when we have allowed our minds to create a situation that was negative. This might have been avoided if we had taken control of our thoughts. Karen's experience began as a normal reaction after losing a job, and she began to shrink her world by becoming a recluse. Whenever we shut others out because we are ashamed or in pain, we set ourselves up for the mind to play tricks on us.

What made this bad situation possible is that Karen was feeling insecure about her age and rejected by the people with whom she had worked. She was unable to look at her layoff from a business standpoint for the firm. The firm was cutting the excess fat from their budget, so anyone who was nearing retirement was the first to go. Instead of entering a spiral of depression, Karen could have considered herself lucky to start the second chapter of her life earlier than she had planned.

Being laid off is one of those situations that can cause us to feel insecure, unwanted and hurt. Yet we could instead assess our many contributions to the job and conclude that the decision was purely a financial move. One of my favorite lines in the movie *New Jack City* would be a good mindset to adopt to move on: "It's not personal, just business."

Are you able to recognize when your thinking is getting in the way? Do you notice when you're responding to life based on what's going on in your head, but you can't seem to control it? Your mind has taken over. Karen should have talked with a close friend or therapist, and devised a plan of action that would or would not include returning to work because she was at retirement age. Choosing this course would have empowered her and allowed her to feel good about herself, albeit unemployed at that time.

Tweaking Your Mindset

One of my all-time favorite books is *The Happiness Advantage*, written by Shawn Achor. The book shares countless stories of famous researchers who proved that changing your mindset changes your reality. The author says that not only does changing your mindset affect how you feel, it also changes the results.

I have a plaque hanging over my doorway that was given to me by a friend, which says, "Queen of Everything." One reason I believe she gave me this title is because I have made it a habit to make the best of any situation. For instance, I hate doing the laundry. So I created the "washing workout." Whenever I have to do laundry, I put on workout clothes and make the workout part of doing the laundry. I walk, run, jump rope or perform some type of calisthenics while I wait for the clothes to wash. After they're in the dryer, I do more exercises.

I live on the second floor of a four-unit condominium complex, so I have to walk about 250 feet to the laundry room, up and down the stairs each time. My neighbors will see me and supportively ask, "Are you doing your washing workout today?" Creating the change in my mindset by incorporating my household chore into a workout, something I love, was ingenious, as no longer is it a burden for me to wash laundry and I lose weight in the process!

Another example of the power of changing your mindset is when two researchers in Achor's book, Ellen Langer and Ali Crum, partnered and performed an experiment using seven different hotels. They told half of the cleaning staff that they were getting more exercise from their work and that their job was providing them with cardiovascular workout and better health. The other half was not told anything about their work. As you probably guessed, the control group that was informed that cleaning and vacuuming burned calories actually lost weight. Not only did they lose weight, but their cholesterol levels also lowered.

The idea that Achor wants us to take away from this experiment is that "the mental construction of our daily activities, more than the activity itself, defines our reality."

Meet La Tasha Langerston…

La Tasha Langerston embodies Achor's principle in every area of her life. La Tasha homeschools her children, and sits on the board of a nonprofit organization for inner-city youth, Urban Born. She is a nationally known public speaker, author and a published columnist in the areas of empowering girls to become women, while helping singles to understand the spiritual aspect of being single.

In the years that I have known La Tasha, I have never heard her complain about the responsibilities that she holds in these positions. She is organized and passionate about matters that involve growth, development and success in both children and women.

La Tasha earned her Master's degree in Business Administration (MBA) from Nova Southeastern University in Florida. It is with this expertise that she created Velvet Steel Consulting, where she provides consulting and corporate training. Equipped with an education that would garner a six-figure job, La Tasha's desire to write and to speak is the driving force behind this socialpreneur. Her first book, *Single But Never Alone*, is a weekly devotional guide for singles.

A former reigning beauty queen, Miss Black California, La Tasha has mastered balancing her vision and creativity with family. She gives back to the community through her tea parties for girls and their mothers and her movement From Girlz II Women. Now happily married with two children, she is currently working on a script for a film that will be a game-changer in the film industry.

Think Your Way There

How you think about your relationships, your career and even your own ability to change your life will determine how successful you will become. Take a minute and think this thought, *"I am wealthy and in perfect physical health."* Really revel in this feeling for a few minutes. How did it feel? Did you feel empowered? Did you feel a little arrogant? Was the feeling liberating? We can literally think ourselves injured like Karen or think ourselves "skinny" like the hotel maids in the prior story.

Your mind is powerful. Focus on what you want, where you want to go, how you want to get there, and who you want to help. Never forget that what you focus on is what you will attract.

CHANGE YOUR THOUGHTS AND YOU WILL CHANGE YOUR ENTIRE LIFE.

Chapter 15
What's Holding You Back?

There are some women who are intimidated by the trials and challenges that present themselves when you chase a dream that is bigger than your current self. If we're going to reach the heights of our talents and abilities, we must learn to listen to the spirit that tells us when to move and not to quit until we have met the goal. Michelle Patterson is one woman who will not let anything hold her back.

In 2014, I finally met Michelle Patterson, CEO of the digital media company, Women Network LLC, and President of the California Women's Conference. Our mutual friend spoke of her in glowing terms, and she knew that I too would fall in love with Michelle because of her tenacity, energy and ability to make things happen. Michelle is a burst of energy and a powerhouse for her cause. She is a woman who inspires and motivates me. Michelle is fun, down-to-earth and a master saleswoman.

In a 2014 article that appeared in the Orange County Register titled "Michelle Patterson Rescued the California Women's Conference—Twice," Michelle recounted raising the $1.8 million to save the conference that Gov. Jerry Brown had cancelled in 2012 due to the California budget crisis. She stated, "It was the most exhilarating, embarrassing, overwhelming, thrilling experience."

Faced with the massive task in front of her, Michelle rose to the occasion. In her words, "I had to put my ego in check and ask for help." Have you decided what you want, why you want it, and what you are willing to do to obtain it? What trade-offs are you willing to make to reach your destination? As with everything in life, you have made trade-offs at every turn. You made a trade-off to be exactly where you are in your life today, and if you are not where you want to be, no worries, you now are positioned to create some strategies and shifts to get yourself into the relationship, the lifestyle, or the financial position that you desire.

Take a minute and think about trade-offs that have landed you exactly where you are. Have you asked for help?

A Bold Start

I have always been a goalsetter. Whether daily, weekly, or yearly goals, it didn't matter. I needed to have a plan of action, and when I set that plan, I was determined to achieve it. One of my goals in life was to become an attorney. At the age of 18, I boldly walked into a law firm without any legal experience and applied for my first legal position with the Law Offices of Kroff & Kagan. Steve Kroff and Ronald Kagan became two of my best school-of-life teachers.

In my initial interview, Steve reviewed my resume. It listed three jobs—Dairy Belle (the local hamburger shop that I worked at during high school), IBM and a title company. After reviewing it, he asked me in his New York Jewish accent whether I knew the difference between a plaintiff and a defendant. With my beauty-queen-pageant winner voice and attitude, I responded that it was apparent that the meaning stemmed from their root words. I told him that the plaintiff was someone with a complaint and a defendant was someone defending themselves against the complainant. Steve told me that he was impressed with my "chutzpah" or in other words my audacious nature.

I was hired and stayed at the firm for two and a half years before moving on to my next position. My tenure at Kroff & Kagan was priceless on so many levels. For one, I met my dear friend Margie Nagel, the legal secretary who trained and taught me how to be a good legal secretary. But the most important lesson I took away from this firm was that I no longer wanted to become an attorney. I knew in my heart that this was not my calling.

At 20 years old, I made a trade-off that would be a very wise decision for a young motherless girl just out of her teens. For over 35 years I have worked within the legal field as a legal assistant/paralegal, and I love the work and my job. It has afforded me the time and resources to live the life that I always dreamed of having.

What about you? Are you aware of the choices that you are making in your life? Do you recognize the trade-offs that you're making? Are you comfortable with your trade-offs?

More Trade-Offs

Of course, I've made other trade-offs in my life and I will share some of them with you. That way you can begin to think about what trade-offs you have made or not made to live the life that you want. I traded my goal of becoming a nun for becoming a mother. I traded an opportunity to dance on Broadway to be a legal secretary, and I traded the single life to become a wife and have a father in my home for my sons.

Some professions require that you give up almost everything. One of them is becoming a trauma surgeon. To date, there are only four female African American neurosurgeons in the world. Dr. Deborah Hyde, a beautiful statuesque woman, is one and she has trained the other three.

I met Dr. Hyde when she hired me to perform at a private party in her home. Months later, I would become her fitness trainer and today we are friends. When I think about trade-offs, she is the woman that comes to mind. Today Deborah works in the trauma unit of a hospital in Southern California. She has won the Patient Choice Award four times. To be an on-call surgeon in a trauma unit is demanding, and she is oftentimes on the clock 24 hours. She has had to turn down many social invitations and sacrifice her own health and well-being to provide her gift to the world. In 1991, she formed the Beacon of Hope Scholarship Foundation for underprivileged youth. For years she and her board members held events to raise money to provide academic scholarships.

What's Your Thing?

What is holding you back? Do you sabotage your happiness and your success? Is there a burning desire in your heart to do something but you don't think that you can do it?

Let's explore how you might be getting in your own way. The first thing that comes to mind is habits that have subconsciously manifested themselves into behavior patterns. The irony here is that the habit can be a good one or a bad one. I have many good habits and just as many bad habits competing for my time and energy. What's interesting is that there are times when a good habit will interfere with a life goal. My love of exercise will cause me to work out with a friend who needs a workout partner when I should be writing. Or I'll spend time coaching someone past the time allotted when I should be exercising.

It's easy to get sidetracked when you have a goal to achieve. But don't get discouraged once you recognize habits, both good and bad, that get in the way of your major life goals and desires. That recognition will help you to position yourself for success.

And once you have learned how to succeed, you can duplicate it with any goal.

Getting this book completed took me seven years. What was holding me back? Well, I would say the first roadblock was the fact that I had never done this before. That made me feel insecure about whether I could write a book. Next, I think I was not disciplined or focused enough, and I didn't want to sit down every day and put pen to paper, the first requirement for all writers. I also think I was intimated because I have read so many really great books, and I wanted my book to be really great too. Also, I think comparing myself with my favorite authors probably played a part in my resistance to write consistently. And finally, I didn't want anyone to judge the book or me.

Ready, Set, Plan Your Success

Don't worry if you feel insecure and struggle with moving forward in achieving a goal or completing a project. This problem can be an easy fix; however, it will take some consistent and persistent work to move forward. You may need the help of wise counsel. It takes a confident person to ask for an honest assessment and to use that information to her benefit. Ask people who know you well, who you admire and respect for their opinions and suggestions about what's holding you back; which areas need improvement; and how you can move forward.

Pay close attention to consistency in their responses and listen for patterns of behavior that others can see that you may not be able to recognize. If most of your close friends tell you that you're always late, then you can conclude that they are probably right. It's amazing what a good friend can help you see about yourself.

Once you have feedback, you can spend some time looking at ways to change negative habits that keep you stuck and turn them into positive ones. Whatever it takes, you're worth it! Stick to your goals.

How do you know when you're accepting a trade-off for the real goal? You will know when you have a goal and your actions don't line up with your dreams. Writers must write. Actors must study and act. Singers must practice and sing. Athletes must perform. Speakers should speak.

In *The Power of Focus* by Jack Canfield and Mark Victor Hansen, they explain that "Your outward behavior is the truth—your inner perception of your behavior is often the illusion." Your actions will tell you what you want by what you are willing to do. The only difference between you and someone who may be living your dream life is that they have applied the behavior patterns to reach their goal. In a nutshell, unsuccessful people have unsuccessful habits, while successful people have successful habits.

Seek expert advice in areas where you are not proficient. A good example is the goal to lose a few extra pounds. It is a simple formula. Decrease the intake of calories and increase exercise to burn fat. *Simple formula, right*? Well, most people slightly decrease their calories and block their success by refusing to add the exercise. If they did, it would ensure their success.

What Will You Choose—Your Dreams or Your Fear?

Our dreams keep us alive and energetic. Age is not a deterrent to achieving our dreams, nor is race or gender. We must continue to persevere with vision and hope to see ourselves at the desired job, to imagine our life in the relationship that we want, and to write checks from our healthy checking account.

How was Biddy Mason able to procure property during a period of time where her race and gender worked against her? She was born a slave and became a nurse and a real estate mogul and also founded the First AME Church in Los Angeles, California. Despite living in the 1800s, she had a dream. I'm sure there was some aspect of her personality/behavior that had to be moved out of the way to reach her success.

For some of us, our fear of success has paralyzed us. We have made up excuses for not becoming who we want to be, and we have given up and given in to living mediocre and unsatisfied lives. As an example of a person who is truly living her dreams, I encourage you to allow yourself to live life to its fullest. Move out of your own way and experience the fear, the uncertainty, and the sheer joy of being vibrantly alive.

In *The War of Art*, Steven Pressfield says that fear is good for us. His theory is that the more afraid we are of doing the thing we desire, the more we must do it. The mere fact that we are afraid should tell us there is something important needing to be done that will move and grow our soul.

THE ROADBLOCK TO YOUR SUCCESS CAN BE FOUND BY LOOKING IN THE MIRROR.

Chapter 16
Discover Your Strengths

So many of us fear that our weaknesses are a negative trait, or we feel embarrassed that we are not good enough to get over whatever weaknesses we are struggling with. Or we fear we are not strong enough to fix a problem that has plagued us for years. As a result, we attempt to alleviate the feeling surrounding our weakness by ignoring it, hiding it, or dismissing it altogether.

Perceptual Defenses

In his book, *Life Strategies*, Dr. Phil talks about "perceptual defenses." These keep you from seeing things that you do not want to be true. They may prevent your picking up warning signs that, if acknowledged, could prompt you to take important and timely coping steps. Perceptual defenses keep you from recognizing that you are falling out of favor with your boss. Maybe this blinds you to the deterioration in your most important relationship, thus allowing further distance and damage to occur. Perceptual defenses can be compared with the pink elephant in the room, which is a metaphor for an obvious truth, issue or problem that is unaddressed or ignored, rather than being discussed.

Perceptual defenses can keep you from recognizing the warning signs of a serious disease that, if detected and treated early, could be contained or cured. Many of us demonstrate perceptual defenses in the area of our weaknesses. We would rather only focus on our strengths. We say to ourselves that it's a good thing to be positive and to look at the bright side of life, not to focus on the negative. I believe the reason people turn to drugs and alcohol is that they are unable to acknowledge their weaknesses. It could be that they lack confidence, are fearful, or simply use it as a means to block out pain of any kind. Whatever the issue is that creates the need to hide, medicate or ignore, it can be eradicated.

Turning Up the Supply

The dictionary defines "weak" as lack of strength. One meaning of the word "lack" is poorly supplied. In other words, your weakness is only a poor supply of whatever it is that you need. A weakness is not negative, unless you allow it to create prolonged negative results in your life. It can be very positive because it can lead you to discover your strength.

Enrou—Teamwork Can Make a Dream Work

I attended my very first live Tedx Talk at UCLA in Los Angeles, California. It was sponsored by TEDxUCLA Women. One of my passions is listening to Ted Talks. They are informative, educational and inspirational. If you are not familiar with Ted Talks, as soon as you finish this chapter, google them and begin the experience of your life. At this event, I was introduced to two amazing young girls, Ann Wang and Jessica Willison, friends since the 7th grade. Their talk centered around their start-up (new business), Enrou, which means en route. Enrou is a one-stop online shopping store that helps developing communities through products made by entrepreneurs in those areas and the money goes back to the communities. Enrou also provides information about the brand or the seller to the customer so they are aware of the company or person designing the goods. They sell fashion accessories, clothing and home décor.

These UCLA alumnae have created a way to strengthen individual, business and global development through their entrepreneurial efforts.

As these young ladies are discovering their own strengths as human beings, women and entrepreneurs, they have made it possible for others to do so as well. Both Ann and Jessica have used their individual strengths coupled with the strengths of their team to create what I call 360 Degree Success, which simply means that every party associated with the project becomes successful.

These girls started with a life-long friendship that grew into a partnership and led to a global business opportunity.

YOUR LACK OF STRENGTH CAN BE OVERCOME, BUT THE DENIAL OF YOUR WEAKNESS WILL BE YOUR DOWNFALL.

Chapter 17
L.O.V.E. and Marriage

It takes an exceptional person to thrive and have a successful marriage. The many facets of a marriage are varied and complex. Just like the athlete who is able to achieve mastery over his body to win the ultimate prize, such is the person who can build a good and happy marriage.

Do you take this man to be your lawfully wedded husband? *Of course, I do, that's why we're here.* Do you swear to live together in holy matrimony? *Yes, I will be very holy and loving and we will do everything together and I will cook dinner every night.* Will you love him, comfort him, honor and keep him, in sickness and in health, for richer and for poorer, for better, for worse, in sadness and in joy, to cherish and to bestow upon him your heart's deepest devotion, forsaking all others, keep yourself only unto him as long as you both shall live? Absolutely!

I answered the above questions in the manner that most of us who have married would respond. We set out on this journey with the full commitment to do these things until real life sets in. In actuality, the reality of the commitment that we make in marriage is simply not commitment. It's more like "I will when you do and I can if I'm happy and I will quit as soon as you make me mad."

The Ultimate Relationship

The idea of living with and loving one person for the remainder of your married life is considered wonderful by many women, scary by some, and utterly ridiculous to others. Marriage is the dream of many young girls. I can remember telling my older sister and her friends about the type of man that I would marry and they laughed and told me that I was delusional because he didn't exist. Accepting my fate, my focus shifted to my dreams to become a model, dancer, writer and psychologist. Being raised by a single parent and hearing my mother's comments about married couples left me thinking that the single life was probably the best one. There was a problem, however. I couldn't help but notice that the women who were married appeared to be happier and nicer. I noticed that the women school teachers who were not married were angry, strict and mean. It was a standing joke for us teens that those teachers needed to get laid.

For most of my adult life, I was not married, but settled for long-term relationships. One was for five years, another one for eight years, and finally six-and-a-half years with my current husband before we were married. If you're wondering if there a difference between being a couple for a long time and being married, the answer is emphatically *"YES."* Does it feel the same being a long-term temporary employee as is does being a permanent employee with benefits?

Marriage is very complex and, in my opinion, it is not designed for everyone. Extremely selfish and self-centered people should not get married, although they do. Many will continue to get married because marriage is the ultimate relationship. And most of us want to experience the love and commitment that marriage is designed to create.

There are so many benefits that stem from being married. You can learn patience, forgiveness, kindness, generosity, selflessness and, most importantly, so much about yourself. Your partner is like a mirror and he will show you exactly who you are. How much you can accept what you see is equal to how badly you wish to grow.

Marriage is for emotionally mature people who are willing to do the work on themselves for the benefit of a relationship. Those who have mastered themselves and have developed discipline, self-reflection and wisdom can enjoy marriage and flourish. Similarly, the people who have learned to utilize a budget, spend wisely, earn a living, use their money for the benefit of others, and operate as good stewards of their resources enjoy financial success. Neither marriage nor money is good or bad; they are what you make them.

A Marriage Requires Work & Attention

I have a very important question to ask those of you who say you want to be married. Are you lazy when it comes to personal relationships? It doesn't matter what type of relationship it is because eventually, after enough time has passed in any relationship, you will begin to treat it like you treat all of your relationships. I am familiar with a wife who neglects her family, her husband and her friends. She does not realize that all of the relationships in her life suffer from a lack of time, energy and effort. I believe that women who don't understand basic relationship etiquette should consider not getting married.

Sharnell Blevins is a woman whose wisdom, guidance, understanding and commitment to her marriage and family and to other marriages are a gift to the community and the world. She is a wife, mother of six children, marriage mentor and writer. In 2014, the Blevins appeared in Ebony magazine in an article titled "The Coolest Black Family in America, No. 41." The Marriage

Works ministry, in which she and her husband are leaders at their church, supports healthy marriage and also provides an extensive pre-marriage counseling workshop for couples.

One of my many theories is that having a marriage is like running a business. In a business, the partners come together for the sole purpose of growing the business, increasing the value of the business, and leaving a legacy. When couples get together, the goals are to build a business (family), increase value by working together (financial), and to leave a living legacy (children/grandchildren). Just as in business, there are many complexities within a marriage that determine its success or failure.

The Johari Window

I attended a women's conference where Pat Ashley, author of *Marriage Is a Blessing*, was a speaker. She made a great observation about marriage. She said that six people show up to get married : (1) The person who you think you are; (2) the person who you really are; (3) the person who you are going to be; (4) the person your spouse thinks he is; (5) the person who your spouse really is; and (6) the person your spouse is going to be.

After I picked myself up off the floor from laughing so hard, I never viewed marriage again in the same light. What she had touched on was not only prophetic, but it reminded me of a concept that I studied in psychology called The Johari Window. The name is derived from the two people who created this model, Joseph Luft and Harrington Ingham. The idea is that various aspects to our personality can be split up this way.

Picture a four-panel window. One pane holds the information about you that is known only to you. The second pane contains knowledge about you of which others are aware, but you cannot see about yourself. The third pane houses those matters that neither you nor anyone else is aware of. Lastly, the fourth pane contains information that has yet to be discovered about you. Keep this model in mind as you try to understand the complexities of marriage and what information will help you make the best decision for finding and keeping your husband.

Remember… You're Part of the Equation

Many of you may be asking what you can do to prepare to be married. And some of you may be wondering whether it's okay if you never get married. Whether you want to get married or not, you may eventually find yourself in a committed relationship. If you want to be happy and enjoy a healthy happy relationship, you must first be happy with who you are, what you're doing, and also have a very clear idea of what you will and will not tolerate in your relationship.

Relationships bring great pain and great joy, and they also require work and effort, time and energy. There are so many variables that determine whether or not they will succeed. Marriage may be for you if you are willing to devote yourself to your growth and development, and then to your spouse or partner.

Is There a Doctor in the House?

Seven years and three children into her marriage, Shelby Lundahl Crouthers went back to school to become a doctor. Shelby, a UCLA graduate, applied to medical school and was accepted at the University of Ohio. She packed up the kids and her nanny, and left sunny California for the cold climate of Ohio. Shelby's husband, a writer, stayed in Los Angeles and commuted back and forth to support the dream of his wife. Today, Shelby lives happily in Los Angeles with her husband and children, and she is in residency at a local hospital.

A strong marriage and well-adjusted, creative children have

been the result of this lady operating very effectively. Of course, not every woman has the skill set to achieve this amazing feat but you have the power, talent and ability to do something spectacular with your gifts.

> **YOUR MARRIAGE IS NOT ONLY WHAT YOU MAKE OF IT. YOUR MARRIAGE SHOWS YOU WHAT YOU ARE MADE OF.**

Chapter 18
Your Joy Is In Your Journey

Have you ever set out to achieve a goal or complete a project, reached the end of it, only to realize that you had been on auto pilot and couldn't remember what you had done or even remember the experience, because you were so focused on the end result?

Every woman who has planned a wedding knows exactly what I mean. You spend countless hours looking for the one pair of shoes that would fit perfectly with the dress; the hours upon hours deciding on invitations; dozens of meetings and conversations to make the big day a success; but you failed to enjoy the time spent with your bridesmaids, your friends, and your in-laws in the process. Your every focus was only on the end result and you've missed the opportunity to relish the journey; the entire experience. If we are not careful, we can move through life with this same mindlessness.

What's Going on Here?

When we make plans to take a vacation, it's very exciting. We decide on the location, whether to drive and savor the trip or catch a plane and get there quickly. Where shall we stay and which airline will give us the best experience? During the preparation, we feel exhilaration at the possibility of being away from our jobs and our homes. We can almost smell the beach as

Chapter 18—Your Joy Is In Your Journey

we schedule a Hawaiian vacation or hear the quiet of a planned trip to the desert. I recently read on an elevator commercial monitor that we get more relaxation and satisfaction from the planning of a trip than from the actual vacation. It said that we relax for months just thinking about the impending excursion. Of course, I had to test this theory so I planned a four-day family trip to Palm Springs. To my surprise, the elevator monitor was correct and I think I know why.

As we're planning the event, we get to experience it in our mind over and over again. Each time we think about it, the scenarios get sexier, more relaxing and more fun. Fast forward to the actual event and what we experience depends on the circumstances that are present the day of the planned event. Why? Because most of us get so bogged down worrying about the little things that we set ourselves up to ruin the vacation that we have been enjoying in our mind for weeks.

For couples, arguments ensue; tempers flare over things like the car not being gassed up before you leave the house. All of the packing should have been done but it wasn't, and now worry begins to set in that you will miss the plane or not arrive at the time you wanted to reach your destination. You get the picture, right? So now everything is messed up. What you say about your vacation later will start with "It was a horrible day." Unrealistic expectations are usually the cause of not enjoying yourself on any journey.

When my husband and I plan a trip, it's always the same pattern. We set a date and a place, and then we both start looking for the hotel, places to eat, things to do. We do this separately, not because we have discussed doing this, but because we both are very proactive when it comes to having fun and planning anything that resembles a party. I have seen couples fight and argue so much during the planning of a trip or vacation that I wonder why they travel anywhere with each other. I know if we fought like that to go on a trip, one of us would cancel it.

What Is the Quality of Your Journey?

Life's ups and downs and twists and turns are the playground in which we learn to appreciate our basic, everyday existence, which at times becomes monotonous and boring. Our daily routines can make us feel stifled, whereas tragedies like September 11th and Hurricane Katrina, in which thousands of lives are lost, cause us to appreciate the little enjoyable things in the day-to-day normalcy of life.

The essence of living the journey is this...It's the pathway to the goal, not the goal itself, that's important. It's the necessary preparation to live out our dreams, such as going to school for eight years, or spending ten years writing a novel, or raising a healthy, happy family before starting on a second career. For me, the real benefit of writing this book has been the courage, discipline and mental fortitude that I've gained in this process. Also, if I didn't write this book, I would feel that I did not honor my own heart's desire—which is a reflection of my authentic self.

In her book *Success Is the Quality of Your Journey*, Jennifer James, PhD states, "Success is every minute you live. It's the process of living. It's stopping for the moments of peace. Success is not a destination that you ever reach. Success is the quality of your journey."

What does the quality of your journey look like? In a high quality life, you enjoy the process that is involved in achieving your goal or learning how to succeed. A big part of success is failure. Learning what is not working is just as important as seeing what is working. When we can make peace with the hard work, the tedious changes and challenges, the uncertainties, the stress, the lessons...all while consistently working toward the dream...

then we will be able to enjoy the journey. It's about living each day focusing only on that day, minute by minute. It's very hard to concern yourself only with the moment you are in. Our thoughts so often drift to the past or the future.

A Different Take

I've noticed that immediately after we set a goal, we become anxious and worried. We overthink the goal and try to talk ourselves out of it because we're afraid. So we focus on the end result in our minds and conclude that we probably won't be able to achieve it anyway. At this point, there's a good chance that we will give up.

However, if we set out to learn more about ourselves, make important associations, and look for ways to make changes in our habits, we can have different experiences. The next time you set a goal, plan what you want to gain and what you may need to learn through your work toward the goal. Do not just focus on the goal itself. Instead focus on what needs to be done to achieve the goal.

For example, let's say that you want to change careers because you are not working in the area of your passion and this has caused you to not live to your potential. You could begin with time alone to determine what you really want to do. When you have made this very important decision, your life has already begun to change, and now you can prepare yourself right where you are to move into your new career. This is how you allow the work to transform you to be your best while on your journey. Then when you reach your destination, you'll have true joy along with the accomplished goal—if it is to be so.

Lisa Coulter—wife, mother, marriage mentor—recently received her Master's Degree in Social Work (MSW) and began work as a Clinical Social Worker at a hospital in Los Angeles. One evening after our marriage mentoring session, we talked about our dreams and goals, and I remember thinking what a lofty goal for a wife and mother. How would she do it? Would her marriage suffer? With three beautiful daughters, would their studies and mommy-daughter time be diminished?

In true Lisa fashion, the answer is a resounding "No." She solicited the help of her mother and husband to balance out her time, and the children grew stronger, smarter and more capable during this journey. Why? Because she was able to experience her journey daily with her family, and because Lisa capitalized on the great teaching lesson that her daughters received watching their mother achieve a life-long dream. She even carved out time to get fit, eat healthy, and kept us informed on Facebook of her trials and tribulations.

Working on an advanced degree is a daunting task for the average person, but it was Lisa's desire to position herself to be the facilitator of a shelter for domestic violence victims. There were times when she was frustrated and stressed out. However, the one thing that this Type A personality would not do is quit. Lisa also wanted to be a role model for her girls. There were nights when she would come home and put up her feet. With a glass of wine, Lisa would luxuriate in the thought that she was tired, mentally drained, and ready to be finished with school, while enjoying the process of the journey and all that it entailed. The beauty of Lisa's story is that when I met her years before, the advanced degree was an idea and a goal—a mere dream, yet unrealized. Today, she is living it.

Our lives should be focused on the joy of the journey. Appreciate the small successes and minor setbacks, be grateful for everything in your life, and see the big picture. Appreciate every day as your preparation for a joyous and successful life. Each day is an opportunity to be happier, to grow stronger, to love more, and to enjoy the journey of your life. Practice does not really make things perfect, but it gives an ease to the effort that is expended because the practice has taught you how to do something better and more efficiently.

Thoughts on My Journey

Some of us get caught up thinking that if we obtain society's notion of the ideal career, that then we will have attained success. We believe that success is the end result. Actually, to confuse yourself with your career is the death of your identity. Yet to enjoy a career that edifies and feeds your spirit and soul is true success. And as this chapter has been emphasizing all along, if we understand the goal of living, we realize that it's the journey that is the most important aspect of our success. What the process does is increase our knowledge, skill, awareness and wisdom and ultimately our confidence in ourselves.

While writing this chapter, I decided to make the completion of this book a journey of joy, a cathartic catalyst to position myself to live my best life near the end of life. Many times we stop dreaming and stop fighting for our authentic lives, whether in relationships or career choice, because we believe we have passed the age for them. We think that since we are 28 years old, it's too late to return to college, or that 40 is definitely too old to find a good husband, or that it's too late in life to make a difference in how we live our golden years.

Some of what I've gleaned from writing this book is that writing is very personal, and that you must be willing to seek and embrace authenticity in doing so. To share your personal stories and allow others to make judgments about your writing style, your grammar and your choice of words is very scary. Yet the joy of doing it far outweighs the fear.

The sheer love of reading, research and writing is filling my heart and my soul with peace and happiness. Whether this book becomes a best-seller or gathers dust on the shelf at the local library is irrelevant in some ways. My journey to become an author is the main event, and each and every day I am savoring the feeling of the discipline and hard work necessary to achieve it. Of course, my hope and desire is that my readers will benefit from all I've shared. However, I have already received so much from the book writing process.

So practice living your dream as you work towards it. And when you reach it, you'll understand that the joy was in the journey.

WHAT YOU WILL BECOME ON YOUR LIFE JOURNEY IS FAR MORE VALUABLE THAN WHAT YOU SET OUT TO ACHIEVE.

Chapter 19
Now It's Your Turn

Are you wondering how you can operate effectively at this stage in your life? Would you like to be your authentic self? To live as your authentic self? You were born with specific gifts, talents and abilities that set you apart from every other person. It is this unique aspect of who you are that attracts people to want to be a part of your life, including those who will love you, and even the people who will hire you. Not being "yourself" can leave you with a void that cannot be filled by anything external. When you deny yourself at your core, there is nothing that will satisfy your soul for long—not a career, not a husband, not a child, not a friendship, not a larger salary or a hobby. Who are you and what is your passion? What do you want others to know about the person that you are?

The reason you begin with who you are and what inspires you is because everything you do in this life reflects the person that you are. Let's pretend that you can hire a marketing company to introduce you to the world. What would they say about you? How will they describe your life? What type of woman do you *want to be*? Classy, edgy, demure, boisterous or sassy?

How do you want to make a living? Do you want to stay at home? Be an entrepreneur? How about being a career woman whose life is focused primarily on her work? Do you want to combine family and career? Are you the jetsetter type? What about an activist with a cause to feed the homeless or change the world?

In what manner do you want to live? Do you see yourself in the limelight? Would you prefer to live in an isolated area and have a quiet life? Do you want to have a family or remain single?

Don't feel bad if you can't articulate this right now. Life is a marathon, and every day is an opportunity for you to explore the essence of who you might be while you start to assess who you want to be. If you already have a sense of yourself and your purpose, then you are positioned to operate at your highest level.

My purpose for this book is to create a movement of women who are committed to growing, healing, educating, supporting, and investing in each other. The power that we possess is only a fraction of what we use, and when our efforts are combined, we are unstoppable. When I think of the individual power of girls and women—such as Malala Yousafzai, Mother Teresa, Oprah, Angelina Jolie and the women featured in this book, I am confident that...

THROUGH L.O.V.E., WE CAN FIND THE POWER TO CHANGE THE WORLD!

Bibliography

Achor, Shawn. *The Happiness Advantage*, Crown Business, New York, NY (2010).

Baker, Dan, PhD and Cameron Stauth. *What Happy People Know*, Rodale, Inc., Emmaus, PA (2003).

Beck, Martha. *The Joy Diet*, Crown Publishers, New York, NY (2003).

Brown, Brene, PhD, LMSW. *The Power of Vulnerability: Teachings on Authenticity, Connection, and Courage*, Sounds True, Louisville, CO (2013), six CD series.

Bryant, John Hope. *Love Leadership*, Jossey-Bass, San Francisco, CA (2009).

Canfield, Jack with Mark Victor Hansen and Les Hewitt. *The Power of Focus*, Health Communications, Deerfield Beach, FL (2000).

Covey, Stephen R. *The 7 Habits of Highly Effective People*, Free Press, New York, NY (1989).

Ford, Debbie. *The Right Questions: Ten Essential Questions to Guide You to an Extraordinary Life,* HarperCollins, New York, NY (2003).

Grant, Tony, PhD. *Being a Woman*, The Hearst Corporation (1988).

Hurnard, Hannah. *Hinds Feet on High Places*, Wilder Publications, Blacksburg, VA (2010).

Huffington, Arianna. *Thrive*, Harmony Books, New York, NY (2014).

James, Jennifer, PhD. *Success Is the Quality of Your Journey* (Expanded edition), The Newmarket Press, New York, NY (1983).

Kay, Katty and Claire Shipman. *The Confidence Code*, Harper Collins e-books, New York, NY (2014).

McGraw, Phillip C., *Life Strategies: Doing What Works, Doing What Matters*, Hyperion, New York, NY (1999).

Monahan, Marta with Jeff Andrus. *Strength of Character and Grace*, Vittorio Media, Los Angeles, CA (2000).

Pegues, Deborah Smith. *Conquering Insecurity*, Harvest House Publishers, Eugene, OR (2005).

Richo, David. *When the Past Is Present*, Shambhala Publications, Inc., Boston, MA (2008).

Schiff, Stacey, "*31 Ways of Looking at Power,*" O Magazine (September 2009).

Smith, Robin L. Lies at the Altar, *The Truth about Great Marriage*s, Hyperion, New York, NY (2006).

Vanzant, Iyanla, *The Value in the Valley*, Simon and Schuster, New York, NY (1995).

The Holy Bible, NLV.

Recommended Reading

Being a Woman, Tony Grant, PhD
Bread Crumbs from the Soul: Finding Your Way Home, Lakiba Pittman
Confronting Without Conflict, Deborah Smith Pegues
Dare to Be Yourself, Alan Cohen
Feel the Fear and Do It Anyway, Susan Jeffers, PhD
Fulfill Your Soul's Purpose, Ten Creative Paths to Your Life Mission, Naomi Stephan, PhD
Hinds Feet on High Places, Hanna Hurnard
How to Behave So Your Children Will, Too, Sal Severe, PhD
I Thought It Was Just Me (but it isn't), Brene Brown, PhD, LMSW
In the Meantime, Iyanla Vanzant
Instinct: The Power to Unleash Your Inborn Drive, T.D. Jakes
Keeping the Love You Find, Harville Hendrix, PhD
Opening Our Hearts to Men, Susan Jeffers, PhD
Single But Never Alone, La Tasha Langerston
Strength of Character and Grace, Marta Monahan
The 7 Habits of Highly Effective People, Stephen R. Covey
The Five Things We Can't Change: And the Happiness We Find by Embracing Them, David Richo
The Happiness Advantage, Shawn Achor
The Joy Diet, Martha Beck
The Pathway of Roses, Christian D. Larson
The Right Questions, Debbie Ford
The Value in the Valley, Iyanla Vanzant
The Writer's Portable Therapist, Rachel Ballon, PhD
Think on These Things, John C. Maxwell
What Happy People Know, Dan Baker, PhD and Cameron Stauth

Acknowledgments

I give thanks, first and foremost, to my Lord and Savior, Jesus Christ, for without You I am nothing. With this project, you have given me my heart's desire. Your grace and mercy saw me through its completion.

To my bishop, Dr. Kenneth C. Ulmer, your honesty and transparency, along with your constant prodding to "go deeper," has taught me to rely on the Word of God for my strength, direction and wisdom; and to my former pastor and spiritual father, Cecil L. Murray, thank you for teaching me that God is not only good but that He created me to be bold and successful.

To my sons, thank you for being consistent in allowing me to do God's work.

Sabra, thank you for always being there when I need you. Your loving support has given me the confidence that I was always covered.

Aunt Pokey, you have been my confidant and my rock. The roads that I have traveled, both good and bad, are paved with your love, support and acceptance and for that, I adore you.

To my "Sistahs" in the spirit, you know who you are. Thank you all for always showing up, listening to my ideas, reading my manuscript, giving me ideas and, most importantly, thank you for your encouragement. Your support of my many endeavors is a testimony to the power of L.O.V.E.

And lastly, to my husband, friend, editor, typist and comic relief, thank you for your strength and support. Our relationship has given me everything I needed to complete this dream of becoming an author. Thank you for loving me the way that I need to be loved.

About The Author

For the past 20 years, Dianne Shorté has been passionately learning from both amazing teachers and from her life, sharing the insights gained with others where she can. Devoted to her community, Dianne has both created and led personal growth seminars in subjects as diverse as financial planning, pre-marital and marital mentoring, physical fitness, public speaking and dance. She is a wife and the mother of three, living in Los Angeles. One of Dianne's true passions is helping other women achieve the lives of their dreams. She hosts an annual "Exhale Party," where women come together to encourage each other to let go of the past and move ahead in their lives. Dianne is available for speaking engagements, workshops, seminars and conventions.